The HAPPINESS QUOTIENT

The
HAPPINESS
QUOTIENT

RITA NAYAR

Also by Rita Nayar
Ordeal By Fire, 2003

Copyright © 2007 by Rita Nayar.

Library of Congress Control Number:		2007906702
ISBN:	Hardcover	978-1-4257-9206-0
	Softcover	978-1-4257-9178-0

All rights reserved. No part of this book may be reproduced or transmitted in any form or by any means, electronic or mechanical, including photocopying, recording, or by any information storage and retrieval system, without permission in writing from the copyright owner.

This book was printed in the United States of America.

To order additional copies of this book, contact:
Xlibris Corporation
1-888-795-4274
www.Xlibris.com
Orders@Xlibris.com
40291

"Rita Nayar has written a fabulous, hopeful book that is essential for anyone on a spiritual path and ready for change. The Happiness Quotient will inspire you, heal you and allow you to feel."

—Susan Hay, Weather Anchor/Television Host,
Global Television, Toronto, Canada

ॐ

"If you are new to spiritual literature, this wise book by Rita Nayar will surprise you for its profound simplicity. If you are already familiar with spiritual ideas of happiness, this book will add to your understanding. Even if you are a real connoisseur, this book will still amuse you in the very least. This writer writes from her heart. One thing you cannot do is to ignore her message."

—Amit Goswami, Professor emeritus,
University of Oregon and author of
The self-Aware Universe, Physics of the Soul,
The Quantum Doctor, and featured on
What the Bleep Do We Know, Eugene, Oregon, US

ॐ

"*Finally,* a book on emotional wellness and spiritual success that makes logical sense! Rita Nayar brilliantly takes us through the topic of spirituality using simple, well thought-out arguments that will easily be understood by the uninitiated. This is a *must read* for anyone starting their spiritual journey."

—Dr. Pawan Goenka, President,
Mahindra & Mahindra, Automotive Sector,
Mumbai, India

ॐ

"Rita shares here the inspiration she received from the Vedanta. This book shows how an ancient philosophy can relate to issues of our daily life and give us courage and strength. Rita's outline of the way to regain inner simplicity deserves compliments."

—Swami Chidananda,
Krishnamurty Foundation, Varanasi, India

ॐ

"Rita, your book is exceptionally simple, but deceptively so, as the important thing is that we allocate time to actively practice your teachings. The world needs your spiritual messages now more than ever."

—Melissa Giovagnoli, President,
Networlding and author of
*Networlding: Building Relationships and
Opportunities for Success,* Chicago, USA

Contents

Introduction 11
Forward 13

Ancient Wisdom 15
Inner Freedom 19
Strength, Fear, and Control 23
Happiness 29
The Nature of Happiness 34
The Mind 39
The World of Matter 46
The Individual Consciousness 51
The Concept of God 55
Universal Laws 60
Maya 63
Desires 69
Karma 75
Reincarnation 79
Good and Bad 83
Values 86
Dharma 89
Meditation 93
Meditative Living 96
Inspiration for Enlightenment 100

A Practical Guide to Starting the Journey 103
Relevance in Everyday Life 109
Relevance to Corporations and Working Professionals 115

My Story 123

Dedication:

To all Gurus, past and present

Om Sri Gurubhyo Namah

Introduction

Ten years ago, my ten-year-old son and husband died due to a horrific tragedy.

One evening, my daughter and I came home from a doctor's appointment only to find our lives turned upside down. As part of a marital discord between my husband and me, he took it upon himself to seek revenge and brutally kill our son, burn down our home, and take his own life. Had my daughter been present, she would have suffered the same fate. But God had different plans for her.

How does one explain away such an incident, especially to the wife and child?

How can one appease the heart and calm the mind under those circumstances? They say time heals. Time only heals if one can intellectually justify what happened, be satisfied with the answer, and accept the loss without guilt, regret, and shame. Time only heals if a feeling of fairness finally envelopes the heart and settles. Until then, there is grief, sorrow, and anger at oneself and others; helplessness and anguish at the consequence; and hopelessness for the future.

My daughter and I have come a long way. Many wonder at our "normalness." There is, however, no magic to this. It has been a journey of profound learning and spiritual growth. They say that life's journey is a preparation for the moment at hand. I feel that God had been intent on preparing us long before the incident happened. For many years before the event, we were provided with spiritual guidance through an ancient Indian philosophy called Vedanta. To this fact of life, I am eternally grateful.

One can argue at the existence of a God, but there is no argument around our preparedness or our overcoming of the tragedy. That in itself proves to me a reason for the existence of a Higher Power, for who can sanely and gracefully overcome horror and senselessness without divine intervention and grace?

And that, in the final analysis, is a compelling reason for me to reveal the secret gems of spiritual thinking.

Forward

It is a primordial mistake! All creatures are looking for happiness in the wrong place. It is like the time when all people used to think that the world was flat. Rita Nayar has written this charming little book identifying properly, the locus of happiness and the means thereby to achieve this thing which has eluded the species from beginning-less time. The book is written with flare and with lucid illustrations; something for those who want to expend leisure time in a more productive or serious way. Taken seriously, it can bring about a complete transformation of personality. Ancient wisdom must constantly be re-clothed in the fashion of the day. Rita Nayar has succeeded in bringing this wisdom in a language most 'modern' readers will appreciate. I wish all happy reading.

—Swami Prakashananda
Chinmaya Mission

Ancient Wisdom

Spiritual living has a very deep and beautiful intent. It invokes in us the image of freedom, love, nobility, beauty, and happiness. It settles in our hearts a quality that makes ordinary experiences extraordinary.

It is said, the one who approaches life in a spiritual manner becomes generous, good-natured, positive, confident, and continually happy. This is because the person revels in the higher truths of life and not in the fickle nature of the world. He knows that goodness will always triumph over evil. After all, it is the unspoken law of the universe.

Recent decades have shifted our vision from quality to quantity. Not only have we compromised on quality, but the pace at which we have demanded quantity has unmercifully multiplied. It seems we are fulfilling most of our wishes, yet quite amazingly, we remain unfulfilled. Satisfied externally, unsatisfied internally. Such has been the interplay of our abundant world outside and our unfulfilled lives inside.

Throughout the ages, the goal of all humanity has been to seek happiness. Although the goal of spiritual life has been to experience that which is beyond the tangible, it is well-known that the *outcome* of this search is unending bliss and happiness. It is the only road that leads to inner freedom and fulfillment. Inner freedom is about being free from the jungles of our mind rather than being free to do whatever we like. Fulfillment is the feeling of not needing anything because we have everything. Who among us would say we have everything? Even millionaires and presidents of nations have impossible desires yet to be satiated! And why do we even need fulfillment? Many of us believe that we are fine as we are. Some of us say, "Really, there is nothing wrong with my life right now. I am fine. All this mumbo jumbo will only get in the way of my progress rather than enhancing it."

Honestly speaking, we have weird ideas about spirituality. We think that we must become a saint or a yogi or a nun and renounce everything in order to be spiritual. Or we think we have to be "goody-goody" and expect to live a very dull life. I hope to God that's not true, otherwise, I will have to call myself dull and boring.

There is nothing further from the truth, I assure you! On the contrary, one becomes very lighthearted, carefree, caring, and confident.

Our current thinking leads us to believe that money, power, status, position, fame brings us freedom and prosperity. The more we have, the greater the freedom. True, money *does* buy us financial independence. Power, status, possessions *do* give us a high. But these are golden chains that subtly bind our minds.

Belief in material gratification and economic advancement comes to us at a cost. We can call these costs a severance from the emotional, psychological side of us where we ignore our inner self. We develop lopsided personalities—either stunted on one side or entirely missing! We sacrifice our own personal development for the sake of material advancement. Most of us die without ever having given it deliberate thought.

Our unbalanced development happens at subtle and imperceptible levels, and cannot be felt, let alone measured. However, we feel its enormous consequences, which come to us in the form of anxiety, frustration, and stress. We then psychoanalyze the reason for our misery and depression and more often than not resort to pills, medication, and doctors. Taking medication is like saying, "Water! Water!" and expecting our thirst to be quenched simply by uttering those words. Pills cannot pull you out of this mess; we need to yank it by the roots! In fact, the price we pay for following this path depletes us in such a manner that if our material wealth ever starts to erode, we have absolutely no psychological foundation to support us.

In other words, we exist at two levels: (1) the functional, material level and (2) the psychological, inner level. At most times, we are chasing the former at the expense of the latter. If we do not address this issue, then sooner or later, this carelessness in living will catch up with us. Lucky is the person who is able to grasp this subtle imbalance early in life.

Here is an interesting thought: if wealth and power gave us happiness, then the CEO of a company should be the most happy, and the person on the lowest rung of the ladder should be the most miserable! So the obvious question is: what is it that gives us true fulfillment?

Our journey needs to begin by knowing the destination, and recognizing it when it is in front of us. To accomplish this, we need a guide. The Olympic winner, the Broadway star, and the financial expert, too, need a coach. In the same way, the spiritual journey needs a guru who has himself attained the Truth. The wisdom of the ancient gurus and rishis (sages) will guide us through this book.

You may think that spiritual philosophy and meditation are irrational and unfounded, even uncivilized in this day and age of information and technology. You may say, "I am an intelligent, logical person: this is not for me!" But as far as my own experience is concerned, and speaking as a professional in a corporate world, I have been delighted at the immense logic in spirituality that the gurus have put together in an effort to truly enlighten our intellect and help us move forward on this unique and awesome path. They are bringing us the gift of inner strength.

This book is intended to give you clear, concise direction on how to achieve happiness despite our busy lives, how to achieve fulfillment without becoming a monk, how to balance economic advancement while uplifting the soul. Yes, one can almost have it all!

Inner Freedom

The intent of every country's law is to protect the rights and freedom of every individual. Legalities are required for social order, significantly different from the freedom we seek as an enlightened being.

There is a wonderful story about freedom. To be free is unquestionably the greatest gift in life. Freedom is sweeter than food or drink; it is more precious than diamonds or riches. Of course, no one these days believes we are not free—at least not in North America! I want to tell you this story because I believe it conveys the type of freedom that we could never imagine!

Once upon a time in ancient India, a king was riding his horse down a country road when he came across an ascetic (monk) sitting under a large banyan tree. The ascetic was sitting cross-legged, chanting a mantra, wearing a loincloth around his otherwise-naked body. The king took pity on this poor creature and stopped his horse.

"Why do you live like this? Why don't you find work and live properly?" said the king.

"I am happy like this, sire. I do not need anything," the ascetic replied.

"I am sure you cannot be happy. How can you be happy when you have no food or clothes or shelter?"

The ascetic made no comment.

"Come with me," said the king authoritatively. "I will take you to my palace and teach you how to live and be happy. You are deluded and ignorant!"

The ascetic was happy to go with the king or to sit under the tree. It did not matter to him. Nevertheless, he mounted the horse and they rode away.

The palace shimmered under the light of the golden sun. The king showered the ascetic with a splendorous big room, servants, and gorgeous clothes and jewelry.

"Now, I will show you how to feel alive!"

A month into his stay, the king offered him a portion of his kingdom and all that went with it—power, possessions, and pleasure. The monk enjoyed the experience of his new life and the months passed quickly. They experienced all the joys of luxury together.

A year passed, then two.

One day the king exclaimed, "I am so glad I brought you here. Now this is life! You and I are free to do what we want!"

The ascetic smiled and said, "Not quite. There is one difference, my dear king."

He went to his chambers, donned his old cream-colored loincloth, and came back.

"You see, I am able to give up everything . . . ," he said, "this is how we differ."

The ascetic's voice trailed away out of the palace gates.

It is clear from this story that freedom is being free from any kind of bondage, not just having the means and the license to do want you like. *It is freedom from want, not freedom of want.* It does not require money or power. The king's vision constrained him even though he had power and money. Freedom requires us not to be constrained by our own mind. To be able to get a coffee on the way to work is not freedom; to be able to sail past a coffee shop without a second thought is freedom. One may have coffee or one may not; the point is that it should not have the power to create agitations either way.

The gurus say that each person is driven by two basic instincts:[1]

1. To preserve what we have, and

2. To gain more than what we already have

I will call these two principles the principle of "gain maximum, lose minimum." Working hard to either preserve what we have or gain more is our impetus for living. This can hardly be called graceful living. It satisfies material fulfillment but cannot satisfy our fundamental need for wholesome living.

When we live by the basic principle of gain maximum, lose minimum, we limit ourselves. Our preconceived notions of success are measured using a yardstick that has been drilled into us over time: that of material success. It was as true for the king as it is for us. If the king's palace ever collapsed, his only instinct would be to rebuild it. Like all humans, he is so engrossed in his little world that he cannot see beyond it.

We are free to do what we want; sure, there is democracy. But the state of our own mind limits us in a way that we do not realize. We chain

---

[1] "YogaKshema" (Sanskrit)

ourselves to habituated ideas that confine our thinking and lifestyle. What use is freedom to a cow that has been tied to a tree all her life? Even if untied, she cannot function outside the radius of her rope! Fear grips all of us who are cornered by our minds in the same way as the cow is mentally confined.

We do not want freedom of will; rather, we want freedom from will. But fear of not gaining or losing objects or beings propel us into action. Millions of memories of past interactions drive us into action without our conscious knowledge. In a confused state of dire want, we reach out to comfort ourselves with a multitude of ego-fulfilling desires. And then we say we have freedom. Nothing can be further from the truth!

The mind is the cause of all our suffering, and the mind is the cause of all freedom.[2] That is the saving grace. The mind that binds us to behave in a certain way is the same mind that can pull us out of it. The mind is our best friend and our worst enemy. That is why, when we conquer the mind, we conquer the world.

---

[2] Man eva manushyanaam kaaranam bandha mokshayoho (Sanskrit).

Strength, Fear, and Control

Inner strength is what makes us climb mountains and leap across oceans. At the core of this immense power lies the ability to attain far-reaching goals without compromising our values. Inner strength is what gave one man, Mahatma Gandhi, the gift of freeing millions of lives single-handedly from an undefeated empire halfway across the world.

The other side of strength is weakness. When we feel vulnerable, helpless, and exposed, we eventually succumb to concessions. Slowly and unknowingly, we yield to compromising our ideals against our wishes and better judgment. Short-term satisfaction goads us despite our belief in patience, fairness, truth, and other values that we learnt in childhood. The pressure to protect ourselves from looking incompetent, unintelligent, humiliated, weak, and disadvantaged is deep rooted. The world thrives, economically and psychologically, on hidden insecurities buzzing anxiously in millions of minds. Accepting events and occurrences that are contrary to what we believe in disturbs our harmony and erodes our strength. The mind, like plastercine or Play-Doh, hesitatingly becomes tamed and trained to adapt to its surroundings. Weakness is another name for fear.

Fear is a great motivator, but it is not fear that makes us climb mountains!

Fear is a burden we carry with us all the time, propelling us to take the next action. It is fear of being poor and dependent that makes us pursue financial security; fear of dying unnoticed that makes us crave status. It is fear of being alone in the future that forces us to pursue or endure a relationship; fear of alienation that makes us follow social conventions. Fear of humiliation makes us dislike people when they contradict our ideas.

The greatest anxieties we face are fulfilling the wishes and demands that define our future. If we were satisfied with the present, we would not worry about many things. But reality is that for most of us the future is insecure, and we spend many hours thinking and planning for it. And in fact, we pay just as much attention to twenty years hence as the very next day!

Fear of the future is based on uncertainty, unpredictability. When we do not know an outcome, our minds stay in a state of frustrated confusion. The mind swings from decision to decision, cries over choices upon choices. For example, supposing we had arranged a picnic, hike, or golf game tomorrow and were told "Tomorrow it may rain," we would spend all of today worrying about the rain tomorrow. The fear of tomorrow is in proportion to the plan: if we had planned an outdoor wedding, the fear would certainly be more pronounced. This lack of predictability causes great anxiety!

Now what about something bigger? What if you were told that you have only a little more time to live and that soon you would die? And you could not predict whether you had two months to live or two years to live?

Predictability is an innate need of the human mind. For the sake of living a comfortable and pleasant life, we look for certainty in every little instance without realizing it.

When we come to work, we expect our papers, phones, and chairs to be in the same place. When we go home, we expect our house and partners to be there. If we send an email, we expect it to reach the other party. We always look for stability. If we buy a vacuum cleaner or a PC, we want to buy the one that lasts the longest. If we purchase a car, we want assurances that it has a good engine. We purchase additional warranty for our appliances, electronics, goods, and services.

When we deal with more subtle things in the world like relationships, we need even more stability. We like to make friends with those who will remain loyal over time. A business partner must stand the test of time in the area of trust and fairness. A life partner is chosen on unconditional love—one who will be with us despite good and bad times, despite our appearance or moods, despite our health or wealth.

In our jobs, we want predictability. Assurances keep us sane and keep the mind calm. In fact, even after death, we want reassurances of where we will be buried and what our afterlife might hold.

So we spend many hours planning for the future and controlling our destiny. But think, *did we ever get the future we planned for?* No! How many of us got what we planned for at the age of twenty, twenty-five, thirty, forty, or even fifty?

The world does not work the way we want it to! *If the outcome were in our hands, every action we have ever taken would have had the desired result.* But this is certainly not the case! The specific results we expected are as unpredictable and elusive as the wind. Although we may generally move in the desired direction, the exact results of our actions are beyond our control. In return, we may get something else we did not bargain for. Seldom do we get exactly what we want.

We must face the fact that we have control over the small things in life but not over big things. We can control the route we take to work, but not the traffic we encounter. We can choose which degrees and exams we take, but not how we will perform. We can choose which medicine to take but not how it may affect us. We can choose whether to have a child but not its future. We can plan and put in all the effort we want, but the outcome is not in our hands.

We have had to react again and again to the unpredictability of life. *This reacting to the outside world again and again makes us weak—we slowly lose ourselves and our convictions. It erodes our strength until we reach a point where we have limited inner strength left and feel as if we are victims of circumstance.* For example, suppose I have a boss who continuously berates me year after year, yet despite all the put-downs, I continue with my job. This ongoing situation will eventually erode my strength and self-confidence. Unwittingly, I have accepted conditions against my will. On one side, we have resigned to our fate; and on the other side, we wait for something good to happen to us. This inharmonious living sounds like torture, yet this is how many of us live. It is fear that keeps us from moving on.

We should be *acting* based on inner strength and convictions, but we actually *react* using formulated patterns.

How free we would be if we could do things without having to worry about the future. How much less disappointment, frustration, stress, despair, and anger we would create if we understood at the outset that we have *limited* power concerning our outer world, and therefore, our future.

We need to realize that, all along, we only make small choices on larger matters that have already been set in motion for us. Certainly, we have very little maneuverability against circumstances in life such as death and disease, earthquakes, or invasion.

In actual fact, we live in two worlds: the inner world of our mind and the outer world of transactions. We have much greater influence over our mind than the world outside. We have the power to change our own self, but not the world around us.

There is a beautiful simile that compares life to crossing an ocean. Crossing the ocean signifies going through life's challenges. For a few seconds, let's close our eyes and picture ourselves alone on a small boat in the middle of the Indian Ocean. There is no doubt it is truly scary. The ocean we know is deep. Strange creatures lurk beneath. God forbid, a storm comes and topples our boat over, for the ocean seems endless in its breadth and depth. A storm may loom, winds may change, and new directions may be set in the course of our journey. Scorching sunrays, growling stomachs, or despondency can consume and obliterate us before we can even see the shore. Life is very much like being in the middle of the ocean. How can I cross this ocean of life, full of unpredictability and insecurity?

Fears expressed in this simile are the very reason we act the way we do. At the most fundamental level, our efforts at living include managing our lives and overcoming uncertainty. To keep afloat in this wide ocean, we make livable boats for ourselves and equip them with a multitude of conveniences. We cram as much as we can into the boats or yachts to ensure we can remain safe and entertained. But because we are so caught up in managing the boat and its contents, we haven't found the time to look up and understand whether we are coming or going. Managing our boat has made our life complicated and stressful, and to a large extent, meaningless. To tell you the truth, a meaningless life is not worth living.

Without long-term goals, we are sure to find ourselves going around in circles. Instead of focusing on the boat, let us refocus our attention on the destination. We certainly don't want to possess everything and go nowhere. We often forget that the boat is merely a means of reaching the destination. In real life, money, status, a house, a car, is only a means for reaching the ultimate goal of true happiness. *It is easy to get caught up in the means and make the means our goal.* If we spend as many hours managing our inner development as we spend in making money, we would all be well on our way to discovering pure happiness.

Now that is meaningful!

Just as every ocean has a shore, every life too has a meaningful destination. We assume that only when we reach our destination will we find happiness and freedom. Our Gurus, however, say that even while being in the middle of the ocean, we can find our true destination. That is the magic and promise of spirituality!

One day, while meditating, thoughts were popping in and out of my mind. Among them was a video I was making for my brother's surprise birthday party. It occurred to me that I had forgotten to call my sister-in-law about a couple of pictures I needed to finish off the project. I almost jumped from my meditation seat to call her, but resisted the urge to. As I continued, it occurred to me how profound a one-liner was that my Guruji had imparted. "Did you know," he said, "that we do not even know what thought will come to us next: that is how little control we possess!" Indeed, thoughts enter our minds rather than us controlling what we think of next.

This is, indeed, mind-blowing! It is true: I have no idea at this very minute what thoughts will come to my mind over the next few minutes. From that day onwards, I understood that there were two things I needed to do: (1) realize that right now, I have insignificant control over my own thoughts and (2) practice awareness of the mind so that I can improve on it over time.

I often hear motivational speakers continuously talk about achieving our ultimate dream, that through drive and motivation, anything is possible. While we need to feel inspired into action, we also need to understand the limits of our ability to control and maneuver. The message of fulfilling the dream is inspiring and born of determination, yet ironically enough, it is focused on economic advancement. We need to shift our attention to fulfilling the dream of achieving personal fulfillment first!

Happiness

Once long ago, a just and benevolent king ruled a large kingdom. He wanted to ensure that every citizen had enough food and shelter and that no one was deprived of basic needs. It was his custom to allow his countrymen to come into the royal court and ask him for things they needed. Walking into the king's assembly one day, a man said, "Dear king, you have provided everything for us. We are very grateful. But I do not have happiness. Please help me." The king thought for a moment, turned to his minister, and said, "This man is unhappy. Please go and find a man who is happy and bring him to me. When our young man here listens to the ways of happiness, he will be happy too."

The minister was sent in search of a happy man. He met a street vendor and asked the vendor whether he was happy. The vendor said he was happy but said, "Go to my neighbor who is a butcher. He is happier than me." When the minister went to the neighbor, he said, "I am happy, but the teacher who lives nearby is happier than me. Ask him." The teacher convinced the minister that the priest was happier. When he went to the temple, the priest convinced him that the king was happier; after all, he had everything. The minister could find no one who admitted to being absolutely happy. He finally came back to the king empty-handed and said, "Dear king, it is you who everyone believes to be the happiest."

What is fascinating about the story is that the thought of being happy did not even occur to the king himself! Being rich, famous, generous, and kind is not a proxy for fulfillment. No one considers themselves to be absolutely happy! For each person, there are times and aspects of life that are not fulfilled.

Most people define happiness as "the state of feeling good," but even happiness is relative. The happiness of a student passing his exam and a student coming first in class is relative. The happiness of a child eating an ice cream cone and a hungry child receiving food is relative. There are degrees of happiness. It is important to note that regardless of this relativity, the desire of the cited individuals is satiated by an external source. What this means is that we generally need an external source to provide happiness.

However, if a person is found to be happy under any circumstance, good or bad, it means that the source of joy is not outside himself. One who is positive, calm, good-natured, and free from fear can also be called happy. To a large extent, this kind of a person sustains equilibrium. In contrast, someone else who reacts to the whims of the world outside experiences a continuous stream of ups and downs. If the environment or external forces are conducive, we are happy. If we do not get what we want, we are disappointed, hurt, and angry. The power of the outside world has the capability to overwhelm us in many ways and control our lives. A truly happy person has the ability to rise above the situations imposed on him by the external world.

Experiencing alternating joy and sorrow and living through constant fluctuations is what makes us human, no doubt, but the outside world is a major factor in how we feel on any given day at any stage in our lives.

So, how does the outside world affect us? The external world is captured by our senses. Every sense organ gathers the experience in the form that they are intended to. For example, the eye captures vision and vision only, the ear captures sound and sound only. The nose, mouth, and skin capture their respective senses. Each captures its own function independently: a sense organ cannot substitute the work of another organ. As the different streams of input come in from the different organs, they gather in the mind. This triggers a memory, and thought is created. The thought will usually make us act or react in a particular manner. These actions and reactions bring about joy or sorrow. Some thoughts will trigger a happy feeling in us, whereas others will bring sadness, anger, frustration, or other negative feelings. The question is, how do we reduce negativity and increase happiness? Where is this happiness or unhappiness coming from?

If we look at the world outside us, we see that the external object does not contain any happiness or sorrow in itself. This is so obvious that it almost sounds absurd. Happiness is not baked into the matter that the object is made up of. For example, a coffee or a car does not have happiness as one of its core attributes. And yet, we feel that if we have *this* car or *that* coffee, we will find happiness. *We need to understand that joy is not an attribute of the thing we wish to possess or consume.* Just think, does the coin in our pocket, the clothes hanging on the shopwindow, or the candies on the counter contain even an ounce of happiness as part of its matter? No!

So how is it that the outside world has so much influence on how we feel? A particular type of food, a certain kind of person or a place, has an intense capacity to make us feel good or bad. How is it that we are so swayed by these external factors? Take a particular item you chose from the menu when dining out. For example, I myself love Cantonese noodles. My friend does not particularly care for them. The joy that the noodles bring me is far more intense than the joy the noodles bring her. So the joy it brings is relative to the person wanting or eating the food and actually has nothing to do with the noodles themselves. The noodles do not contain any magical property but are the same regardless of who eats them.

This is important to know because we are trying to discover the source of happiness. While it seems obvious that objects do not contain this quality of happiness, we seem to think that contact with a particular place, person, or thing brings us happiness or unhappiness. Gurus will say it is false thinking!

An important conclusion, then, is that happiness is not to be found outside but to be found within. In fact, we can take this line of reasoning a little further to make this thinking foolproof.

If happiness was in the object outside of us, it should give us happiness all the time. Whether I drink the coffee now or later, it should have the same effect. But coffee can give us happiness now and cause "sorrow" later. Sometimes we want coffee, and at other times, we do not. This is very true of relationships. If someone gives me happiness now, the same person should give me happiness not only anytime but every single second of my lifetime. If chocolate ice cream gives me happiness now, it should give me happiness at any given time as well.

If happiness is in the chocolate ice cream, then I should be able to eat ten ice creams, and each should give me the same pleasure. The tenth ice cream should be just as desirable and delicious as the first one I ate. But we know this is certainly not the case.

In addition, if happiness is in the object we desire, then that object should give everyone the same happiness. But this is definitely not true. Chocolate ice cream is only liked by some, not all. A skiing trip or a new movie that was released last week will be chosen by some not all. In fact, why are we applying this logic to tangible things? It can hold true for intangibles as well. Ideas, concepts, or even relationships do not contain happiness as an attribute.

A relationship that we want badly should give us the same happy feeling all the time whether it is the first day, the fiftieth, or the five hundredth day, whether it is morning, noon, or night. In fact, if happiness was "baked" into the matter of that person, that person should be able to provide everyone the same happiness he or she provides me. Ten similar relationships should also give me ten times the joy. But we know this is ridiculous.

So again, the important deduction is that happiness is not outside in an external object or person or a circumstance. Objects, events, and people are what they are. *It is our experience with them that gives rise to joy or sorrow. And the imprint it leaves on our minds is what makes us want to go near or move away from them a second, third, or nth time!*

There is a story about a security guard who used to watch the CEO drive in every morning through the company gates. The CEO rode in the backseat of a limousine, sometimes folding his newspaper as he approached the building. The guard envied the driver, thinking how wonderful it would be to sit in the air-conditioned car and drive such an important man. The driver used to drop the CEO off on the front steps of the building. He could picture the receptionist sitting inside, sipping her coffee, and talking to very important clients on the phone. He wished he were the receptionist. As the receptionist watched the CEO come in and talk with the office manager, she thought of how lucky he was shaking hands with the top guy and engaging in important conversation. As the office manager ushered the CEO into the conference room, he wished he was making the very important decisions instead and getting paid big money for it. The CEO stared out of his ninth-floor executive suite and thought about how simple it would be to be a security guard and not have to worry about a million things!

Now we can say with great conviction that happiness is not existent in things external to us. Happiness is not part of external matter but is part of our inner self. In actual fact, gurus have discovered a wonderful thing about happiness! They say that happiness is actually intrinsic to us: it is our very nature. The glitch is that we do not know how to tap the happiness hidden within. In later chapters we will see!

The Nature of Happiness

Our normal definition of happiness is somewhat different from the one that is used in spiritual philosophy. In our current state of understanding, happiness is that which creates excitement, exhilaration, joy. For example, transitory joy can be found in sipping a cold drink on a hot day, reading our favorite book, or watching an old television show. Joy can be found on vacations, in winning the Olympic medal, or in having sex with our lover. These types of activities create a feeling of elation while they last. In fact, the aftertaste they bring can often stay with us for quite a while.

Happiness in the spiritual context is different. Happy-ness is regarded as Bliss[3] and is accepted only when it meets the requirement of being permanent. In other words, if the state of "happiness" can come to an end, it is not considered happiness. For it to make the mark, happiness must fulfill two related conditions: it must be permanent and it must not be false. A false thing can be negated or destroyed. Something permanent cannot be negated or destroyed. "With something that is impermanent," the Gurus contend, "how can one find continuous, permanent happiness?"

---

[3] Anand (Sanskrit)

A finite action must have a finite result. Whatever we pursue in terms of "doing" has an end. Even if I do something for the longer term, it has an end when the desire gets fulfilled, completely or partially. For example, the activity of eating mango ice cream or flying my glider will come to an end. Going to Mexico on a vacation is a finite action with a finite result. Putting money away in the bank may seem longer term, but it too is used for some finite purpose. So is watching a movie, kissing a partner, going to a party, etc. *Momentary happiness, however prolonged, is not good enough because in between our bouts of delight, we experience "suffering" in the form of unfulfillment, insatiability, anxiety, stress, distress, troubles, and sorrows. In between our bouts of happiness is anxiety about the future or a force of the past.*

For each of us, secular happiness comes and goes. Some of us have more or less than our share compared to others. When each positive experience is over, it leaves us wanting more. Because we long to relive those experiences that caused pleasure, joy, or delight, we pursue those activities in a repeatable pattern. However, in this continuum of planned and unplanned activities are felt gaps of unhappiness. From one action, we move on to the next, gathering the string of joys. Like Christmas tree lights, the bulbs light up while the string holds them together! If we do not get to the next action as planned, we become frustrated and stressed. Whether we get what we want or not, our energies and anxieties are focused on either "what can be" or "what could have been." *Both the past and future persecute our mind. This is termed as "sorrow and suffering" by ancient wisdom.*

Our goal, in actual fact, is to be happy under any circumstances. No one looks for unhappiness as we already know. Temporary happiness comes and goes with certain activities, but in permanent happiness, we do not have to continuously look for "the next thing" to amuse and occupy us.

Ancient wisdom declares that happiness is instinctive to us. No one needs to coach us on how to be happy. We certainly know when we are.

Everything in nature tries to retain its natural tendency or predisposition. For example, it is the nature of the sun to shine, it is the nature of fire to burn, it is the nature of sugar to be sweet, it is the nature of a rock to keep still. In the same way, it is the nature of any living thing to be predisposed to happiness. For example, left at room temperature, water's natural inclination is to be a liquid. Just as it is the nature of snow to be cold, in the same way happiness is the nature of man, his *dharma. It is the state most natural for man, and it is proven by the fact that happiness is what we gravitate towards.* Even a man who commits suicide wants it for his own happiness, thinking, "Oh, I will be so happy when this goes away." We cannot give up this desire for happiness because we did not initiate it. It is a natural phenomenon.

Some people want to be happy but unknowingly create misery for themselves. Once, there lived a priest who was an avid golfer. He woke up one Sunday morning and decided that it was such a beautiful day that he had to get in a round of golf. But he was due for a sermon so he told his assistant to fill in for him and tell the congregation that he was sick. When God learnt of the priest's activities, He smiled to himself. God's assistant said, "You must teach him a lesson, God. The priest cannot be allowed to get away with this!" The priest played the first four holes like a pro. Said God's assistant, "I don't understand. Why are you letting him play so well?" God simply smiled. The priest continued on, demonstrating fantastic skill. He was ecstatic and couldn't believe he had so much talent. On the final hole, he made a hole in one and could hardly contain himself. God's assistant was puzzled, but God knew what He was doing. When the game was over, the priest wanted to share his amazing accomplishment at the golf course. Unfortunately, he could tell no one!

While we do not need instruction on how to be happy, we do need instruction on how and where to find it.

I remember times when I have wanted to repeat a personal experience because it was so gratifying. But what an effort it was trying to maneuver the world in order to recreate the scene I wanted! Whether I craved for loving words, a particular gesture, a feeling of elation, or just plain and simple peaceful moments, I consciously and unconsciously tried my best to create the outcome. Most of the time, manipulation of the world to our way of thinking is an impossible task. We finally end up settling for second best.

A very interesting behavior of all humans (not of animals, mind you) is that peace and happiness are very often postponed to the future: "When I do this, when I achieve this, when I possess this, I will be happy." This is absurd, but it is what many of us do!

A child looks forward to his birthday the whole year. When time draws near, the child starts planning his party. He tells his mom he wants Andrew, Max, and Atul to come. He wants a Spiderman cake and Spiderman loot bags. On the morning of his birthday, he can't wait until party time. At party time, he can't wait until he blows the candles. When the fun and games are over, he can't wait until he opens his presents. When he opens a present, he can't wait until he opens the next one. Do you see a pattern?

The grown-up is no different. With constant energy deployed towards the future, whether it is the next day or the next week or the next month or the next year, we create a mind-set where we postpone our happiness. We cannot wait "until I go on vacation", "until I am at my cottage", "until my night out with friends", "until I retire" to be happy. We hardly ever find ourselves at peace at that particular moment in the present.

Really speaking, both the past and future are only possible in the present moment. They have no meaning unless thought of in the present and therefore are only a play of the mind. They are as unreal as watching a movie or television. Since the future can only be created in the present moment, pay attention to the present.

Postponing happiness for the future makes little sense when we take into account our earlier discussion regarding the limited control we have over the outer world or the events that we will have to face in our lifetime.

We must learn to be happy in the current state without requiring some criteria or condition to be happy.

In no way does this mean we should not plan our futures or care about it. It does mean, however, that once our energies have been depleted in planning the action, we must let it take its course. When we are constantly wasting our efforts on the means, we forget the simple goal of happiness. We have little time to reflect on life; and without reflection, change in one's own thinking cannot occur.

A restless mind should be developed spiritually so that the inner personality is transformed to one of inner fulfillment and happiness.

The Mind

The obvious place to look for happiness is in the mind. But wait! The mind is a wonderful instrument; it can throw us in the deepest depths of despair and raise us to the highest point of elation. At a moment's notice, we can be on top of the world, or a sudden small word, gesture, or obstacle can throw us instantly in a downward spiral. Let us continue our journey of discovering happiness and delve further into the fascinating realm of the mind.

Can we bring about a state of mind that is peaceful, tranquil, joyous, and that does not get disturbed? Each day has its ups and downs; we cannot escape circumstances. Sometimes a simple phone call, gesture, an insult, or a tug of the memory throws us off balance. Sometimes it's as mundane as dinner getting ruined or taking the kids for soccer practice that annoys us. These problems can be viewed as different nuisances on different days; but somehow, when we have to live with them day after day, they begin to feel overwhelming. At some point, they rouse in us a sense of disappointment, anger, or frustration with the world and create a feeling of resentment and helplessness. When we cannot change the world the way we want it, we either succumb to it or become rebellious. These cumulative circumstances under which we adapt and survive create a lifetime of irreparable damage. They distort our judgment and affect our ability to think clearly. Our vision disappears; our focus in life becomes shortsighted. Sometimes it seems that there is no answer: nothing we can do to change the circumstances. But there is nothing further from the truth!

We are empowered beings. Do you know why animals walk on fours and man is a vertical animal? Because for creatures, the functions of the head, heart, and sexual organs are on the same horizontal level. Man, on the other hand, has been privileged with a crown of intellect, and with a heart that sits above the sexual organs. Spiritual thinking is the only force that advocates this order. Spiritual living is the only way to gain sustained courage and confidence. The material world can topple us over in an instant, but once having developed our inner core, nothing can ever shake us.

In India, there is a story about a lover. He pined for his beloved, for it was unrequited love. He begged and begged her to become his bride, but she refused him over and over again. One day, she decided to do something about it and said to him,

"Come and meet me in three months time. I will be at such and such a cave in the Himalayas."

The ladylove took off for the foothills and started living in the cave. For the young man, three months seemed like three years. Finally, the anxious lover came to the entrance of the cave. There he met a frail woman with untidy hair, yellow teeth, body thin and weak from hunger, taking the support of a walking stick. Flesh hung below her droopy eyes.

"I am looking for my beloved. She told me to meet her here. Have you seen her? She is young and beautiful!" The frail thing looked into his eyes. And full of compassion, she said the following words to him,

"Do you *still* want to be with me? You were attached to an image in your mind. Now go home and do not get deluded by the world."

There are various hidden implications in this small tale! It is about the mind, about permanence, about delusion, about reality, about love and lust, and about understanding the world from a broader and deeper perspective!

The mind is like a pure, clean crystal made of the finest, most delicate material. It is so subtle and sensitive that the minutest of vibrations or hues can be picked up. It is a million times more sensitive than the finger, tongue, or eye that can feel the presence of the smallest foreign particle. In fact, it has a far greater range compared to the senses because it is so subtle. (This Vedantic mind is not to be confused with the western "brain," which is a physiological organ.)

A crystal reflects whatever is near it. If the crystal sits on a blue jacket, it takes on a blue hue; if it is close to a red scarf, the crystal reflects red. So too the mind takes on the quality of the things around it. Just as the crystal can equally reflect a knife or a gun as well as a gorgeous flower, so too the mind can reflect good and bad. Reflection, in this context, means that the mind absorbs and gets affected by whatever is in front of it. We can see this in small children when they learn to imitate. This is how and why we get so influenced by our environment.

To build inner strength of the mind is not to be influenced by its surroundings. However, this impact of the outside world on the mind can be used to our advantage. Because the mind can pick up the slightest of aspects, it is capable of grasping spiritual concepts too. Uplifting our mind is the only way to end unhappiness and attain fulfillment.

When the mind picks up anything from the environment, positive or negative, a certain impression (samskara) is formed. We have been picking up samskaras since the day we were born. Every little experience in our lives has created unseen, undetectable, discreet impressions, which later become the impetus for our actions.

Our eyes see innumerable objects, but we do not absorb everything we see. We may be at an art gallery and see many things: paintings, speakers, guards, people, pillars, ceilings, etc. What we will gravitate towards are those thoughts that we hold very dear, those that are deep-seated and embossed on our psyche. So some of us will gravitate towards the architecture, some of us to particular types of paintings or sculptures. Significant thoughts are nurtured constantly by our minds, retained, and become part of our core being. By significant thoughts, I mean those thoughts that are more important to us, thoughts that we pay more attention to and affect us.

The outer instruments with which we see, hear, taste (i.e., the eyes, ears, etc.) do not get attached; it is the inward instruments of the mind that gets attached to ideas, notions, emotions, likes and dislikes, etc.

Impressions resurface when our sense organs come into contact with associated people, places, or things. Our very first impression should be neutral, but due to the storehouse of effects that we have accumulated, it is rarely so.

These samskaras drive innate desires. These subtle tendencies are called vasanas. It is through the filter of our good and bad vasanas or predispositions that we perceive the world. The external world is understood by us in the way that our limited mind interprets.

Each of us may look at the ocean, but in us will arise different thoughts and sentiments. An artist will behold beauty, an explorer will dream of adventure, a marine biologist will analyze microorganisms, and perhaps you and I will simply admire and enjoy. In the same way, all perception of the outer world is dependent on and congruent with the individual mind. Along with our thoughts of various objects come emotions of joy, sorrow, love, hate, etc.

There are only two outcomes of any impression: moving towards or moving away[4] from that which we come into contact with. Our feelings

---

[4] Pavratti and nivratti (Sanskrit)

move towards either love or hatred. With this swing of the pendulum, we move away from certain people, places, and things; or we are attracted to certain people, places, or things. *We either seek or reject, approve or disapprove, take or refuse, grab or discard, confront or avoid. My judgment in the future will be based on my earlier impressions, my likes and dislikes, imagined or otherwise.*

This emotional realm of likes and dislikes runs our lives, and every thought and action is propagated by these reactions.

Sometimes thoughts and action will be at odds with each other. While what we think and what we feel should be in sync, many times what we do and what we want to do are different. This creates discord in our personality and is a major cause of stress, frustration, and depression. Not being allowed to be ourselves causes great anxiety. For example, I may say, "I should not eat these fatty peanuts," but I do. Now I have created a rift in my own personality because what I do is different from what I should do. I have caused my mind to become agitated because I have compromised myself. Using another example, if I say "I will call you back" and actually do not want to call you back, I create a fear in my future and hope to never bump into you again. Unharmonious personalities are dangerous to our health since they detrimentally affect the mind and consequently our bodies.

When we act, prompted by our vasanas rather than being guided by the knowledge of what is right or wrong, we strengthen these likes and dislikes, which constitute the impurities of our mind.

Likes and dislikes run our lives. They bind us, condition us. When we think of freedom, we now see that doing whatever we want is not freedom. Actually it is quite the opposite. *Doing what we are conditioned to do is binding.* Our perception of the world has been derived not from good judgment of right and wrong, but from our past actions. We keep strengthening our likes and dislikes due to culture, newspapers, media, friends, parents, teachers, movies, advertising, and whatever else we come in contact with.

When we understand how our own mind behaves, we can infer the same for all other minds. They too are conditioned by their own likes and dislikes. They too have handcuffed themselves to their own little world.

We do not control the mind; rather, it controls us! We are at the mercy of our own creations. Because of our mind, we become angry, jealous, lusty, greedy, selfish, arrogant, deluded. These kind of emotional attributes are called impurities of the mind.

In order to gain mental peace, we need to remove these impurities or negative emotions and tendencies; otherwise, they will get more entrenched as time goes on. There is no doubt that the freedom we seek will be more difficult to gain as time progresses because our habits and ideas get further ingrained in our psyche. Without discrimination, we cannot change; and change is not possible for the one who is not aware of his or her mind and its nuances.

Ancient wisdom says "right thinking" is the key to purifying the mind. It is the same mind we use to become great, noble, cheerful, and calm; and the same mind that dwells on negativities. Just as we manage the same body to be fit or unfit, we have to manage the mind to be pure or impure.

Like a small child who wakes up every morning, the mind too starts its activity upon awakening. Flitting from one thought to another, it dances about without hesitation. Just as a child may ask a hundred different questions in one breath, the mind too bounces from one topic to another. When it finally rests on a particular priority, it instigates an action.

All action is thus based on thought. Since the quality of an action is based on the quality of the thought, it is very important that we pay utmost attention to how and what we think. As we think, so we become. Reconditioning the mind or undoing previous habits of likes and dislikes, preferences and prejudices, is the start of finding true happiness.

Every thought and action continues to strengthen our core personality and develop our persona. If we are aware of the nature of our mind, we can consciously create a life for ourselves free from anxiety and stress, full of rich understanding and fulfillment.

Using the very same stressful mind to determine how to make itself happy will be the challenge we should be ready to undertake in the remainder of the book! Though gurus and texts are available to guide, each of us has to undertake this journey on our own.

Only you can lift yourself!

The World of Matter

Our discussions up to this point have been on the individual self: freedom, control, happiness, and the mind. Let us keep moving on in our search for happiness by exploring the world.

The ancient sages claimed that in the world there are only two things: matter and Spirit. It is easy enough to explain what matter is, but to explain what the Spirit is, we need to start by defining matter. Then, through a process of negation, saying, "It is not this matter. It is not that matter", we can come closer to seeing what the Spirit is.

Matter is easy enough to distinguish. At first glance, anything visible and concrete is matter. But there are several other attributes that help determine the nature of matter.

One quality of matter is that it cannot know of its own existence. For example, a table or chair cannot know of its own existence. Nor can matter know the existence of another piece of matter. The chair cannot know the existence of the table, nor can the table know the existence of a chair. Matter does not have self-awareness as its principle. We are not questioning whether matter exists, but matter itself does not know it exists. Something else knows it exists. Our bodies too are considered matter: my arm does not know of its own existence. My eye, my toe, my tongue, my heart do not know of their own existence or the existence of the organ next door. A dead body does not know of its own or another's existence.

Another quality of matter is that it comes and goes. *All matter has a beginning and an end.* A clock, an apple, a tree, a wave, a gust of wind, and even a mountain has a beginning and an end. There are no exceptions. Each cell in the body has a beginning and an end. Our total body, in part or in whole, has a beginning and an end. Matter is "born", exists for a period of time, and "dies." It was nonexistent before and will be nonexistent again. Its existence may span a day or may span a hundred million years, but at some point, matter will dissolve.

Matter is also said to be changing continuously: it modifies into something else with time. A wave changes to froth, froth changes to water. Fruit falls to the ground and becomes soil. Wood burns to ashes, stones become dirt, seeds become trees. Oceans dry up and become land. Planets break up and become asteroids. Hairs grow, decay, and fall. Teeth grow, teeth fall. Cells grow, cells decay, cells die. Nothing ever disappears. Matter simply changes form and is called by a different name. So while we say that matter was nonexistent before and after, we really mean to say that it simply keeps changing form. It moves from gross to subtle, subtle to gross, or manifest to unmanifest, and unmanifest to manifest.

All matter has name and form. Matter comes with a form and we give it a name. All forms are limited by time and space, meaning that all matter occupies a certain timeframe while it exists and occupies space, no matter how subtle. Matter cannot exist without the concepts of time and space, since all creation depends on time and space. A can of soda, the tip of a needle, a banquet hall, or the Pacific Ocean occupies space. No matter how small or large, they also stay only for a period of time.

Matter can be gross, or it can be subtle. All matter can be divided into one of five elements: space, air, fire, water, and earth. All matter fits into any one of these categories or a combination of these elements: wood or anything concrete is referred to as "earth", any liquid fits into "water", any type of heat is "fire", all gasses are "air." The subtlest of these attributes is space, and the grossest of these attributes is earth.

Space and air are considered to be matter even though they cannot be seen or heard with our eyes or ears. The subtler something is, the more pervasive it is, and the finer it is. It can spread far and wide and cover solar systems and galaxies.

Space is subtler than air, air is subtler than fire, fire is subtler than water, and water is subtler than earth. Earth is the densest and grossest of all.

When looking at our own bodies, we find that our body is made up of matter: we have combinations of air, fire, water and earth, and space in the form of flesh, blood, oxygen, etc.

In our search for happiness, we are looking to find the source, and certainly, we are trying to establish that all this matter we have talked about does not have happiness as its property. *Because the external world does not contain happiness as its attribute, matter can never be the source of joy.* While we may say that the tongue tastes and it enjoys food, the sense is temporary. The tongue cannot even taste itself. *Something else is enjoying the tasting; something else is enjoying the beauty in the flower, not the eye.* The tongue and all other senses are merely instruments through which we experience the world.

Our bodies operate at three levels: the physical, mental, and intellectual. From the grossest to the subtlest, the three layers of the body can be described as follows:

- The gross body is that part of the body which can be seen and is constituted as flesh, skin, bones, blood, etc. It includes all organs and systems that function and govern the body.

- The subtle body consists of our mind, our thoughts, our personality, our memories.

- The causal body is subtler still. This layer contains latent elements of our vasanas and is responsible for the manifestations of a specific personality.

Although this subject has been minutely examined by many ancient rishis (sages), it hardly matters exactly how we dissect the layers of the body. The point is that from the grossest to the subtlest parts of the body, they are all considered to be matter. The nose can smell various scents but is not attached to a specific smell. The eyes are not attached to one color. The mind is not attached to one emotion, nor is the intellect attached to one thought. This means that they are not owners but are mere instruments. Otherwise, the chair would say, "Why are you sitting on me?" or a thought would hold on as long as it wanted.

How can we say that the mind is matter? Does it fit the criteria of the quality of matter? The mind is made up of thoughts. We have all different types of thoughts, one after another. Each thought is born and each thought dies. Thoughts come and go. Thinking is nothing but a string of related or unrelated thoughts. Like each frame of a movie that gives the illusion of movement, thoughts too are strung together to seem like thinking is alive. Thoughts are not aware of anything. Each thought does not know of the existence of another thought. We have so many different types of thoughts: intellectual thoughts, emotional thoughts, sentimental thoughts, angry thoughts, etc. Thoughts change faster than the speed of light. In our thoughts, we can go to India and come back in less than a split second. So we say that the mind keeps changing. Because of all these factors, mind is considered to be matter albeit subtle.

The mind is a unique instrument owned only by humans. It has qualities not manifested anywhere else and has the following functions:

1. uncertainty or fluctuation where *the mind* cannot decide and is in a state of flux;

2. decision, which is the ability of the *intellect* to come to a certain conclusion;

3. *memory*, which remembers the storehouse of all impressions, gross or subtle; and

4. *ego*, which functions as the "I" and "my" thought.

Whenever we come into initial contact with an object, an instant fluctuation is encountered. At that moment, the mind is uncertain of what it has perceived. We cannot determine how to react. Or we may not be able to understand what the object is or what the object is doing here. This may last for a split second. Then, as we start to dip into our memory banks, our intellect starts reflecting on the situation, and we come to a determination. This is the point where the intellect is functioning. The intellect comes to a halt and has made a decision based on the storehouse of memory and impressions.

Each of these three functions is propelled and supported by the word "I." This is the ego and is the reference point we use for ourselves. This ego is embedded deep within us and is the hardest to manage. *It creates havoc by identifying itself to whatever it sees, hears, tastes, smells, or touches. It automatically relates everything to itself. It is what creates in us our sense of differentiation and individuality. It divides us from the rest of the word. The "I" and "my" thoughts are aspects of the mind that are going to be crucial in moving beyond.*

Collectively, these four functions are responsible for our behavior. Actually, our entire future. If we can understand the workings of our mind, we can make or break our future. We can make ourselves happy or miserable. We cannot avoid what external events happen to us, but we can certainly develop the ability to become happy through subtler thinking. We cannot stop it from raining, but we can certainly carry an umbrella.

In the next chapter, we will cover Spirit.

The Individual Consciousness

If happiness is not to be found in the external world of matter or in our material body, then we need to keep searching for the source of our happiness.

The whole world is full of matter. Anywhere we look, we see inert objects surrounding us. We can see objects, hear objects, feel, taste, and smell objects through our senses.

If I see the world full of matter, I must ask the question, who is doing the seeing, hearing, tasting, etc.

In any interaction we have with the world, there are two entities involved: the subject and the object. In other words, there is an experiencer and the experienced. The knower and the known. Understanding their roles is very important in differentiating between the two, and finally in discovering the source of happiness. In fact, what we will find on this journey is our own selves—something that many of us have been searching for all our lives! We really do not know who or what we are!

In our day-to-day interactions, we say, "I eat an apple", "I play baseball", "I see a movie", "I drive a Toyota", "I love my coffee", "I hate spinach." In every one of these expressions, there is a subject and an object. We may do or feel many things, but the "I" is constant. The world is varied, but we are only one experiencer, one knower knowing the known.

The knower of a thing is different from the thing known. The owner of a thing is different from the thing owned. The mind, which is a known entity, is different from the knower of the mind. The owner of the mind is different than the mind.

This inquiry into "who am I?" is what we must pursue to discover the Spirit. We already know that we are not the inert body or the mind or the intellect. We know this because we can say *my* mind or *my* *intellect*. If we use the word "my", we have to ask ourselves whose mind and intellect are we talking about? Who possesses this mind and this thought?

There is no doubt that matter does not know of its own existence. All matter is simply a combination of elements. So we need to ask, who knows of their existence? It is "I" who knows. I am aware. I am aware of my own existence and that of everyone and everything else. This awareness is what makes us sentient or conscious. That is the big difference between matter and spirit. Spirit is sentient or conscious and matter is not.

The "I" is none other than the Spirit! We are the pure Spirit. We are not the eyes, nose, ears, neck, stomach, feet, etc. I own these limbs and organs as possessions but it is not me. I *have* a body as opposed to I *am* the body. The nose is breathing not for its own sake but for the sake of the spirit! The eye is seeing not for its own sake but for the sake of the spirit, and so on.

Each one of us is conscious and aware. We know we exist. We are. We are all different people and creatures, but we all have this innate force of sentiency that is common. I cannot deny my own existence. Even as I deny my existence, I am confirming it by saying *I* do not know.

This awareness has been with us since the day we were born. I know I existed when I was ten years old, and I still exist at this present age. The body and mind are undergoing constant changes; but the I, the Spirit, ever remains the same. It is the reason we always feel young and the reason we all feel immortal!

The experiencer or "I" resides in the body and is referred to as the Atman.[5] Atman is pure and unadulterated by our mind and thoughts. As Swami Vivekananda so beautifully expresses, "We are not human beings with spiritual experiences; we are spiritual beings with human experiences." Atman experiences the world through the body. The body is a covering, a medium through which our Atman expresses itself. To express itself, Atman must go through the filter of the mind.[6] We see through our eyes and act and react to the perceived world through the filter of our minds.

In order to view the world from a spiritual standpoint, the filter of the mind must be cleaned; and the mind made to be pure and steady, unpolluted, and aware-full. The surface of a glass needs to be clean before we can see through it. *In the same way, the mind must be clear before our Consciousness or Atman or Spirit can shine through. It is the mind that interferes and makes us miserable. The conditioned mind, its vasanas and tendencies, creates havoc.* It seems we cannot manage the mind, it manages us.

The serene, blissful Consciousness (Atman) is not affected by the world outside. In itself, the Atman is Pure Brilliance, Pure Radiance, Pure Awareness, Pure Existence. It is Self-Luminous, Self-Operative, Self-Knowing. In other words, it does not need something else to exist or to prove its existence. Just as a small cloud in the sky can obscure the mighty sun, so too our tiny mind hides the mighty Atman!

We need to know that we are the Pure Spirit, the source of all happiness. We are not a conglomeration of the body-mind complex. The

---

[5] Atman (Sanskrit)'
[6] Antahakarana (Sanskrit)

"I" we refer to is the Atman, the Spirit. Somehow, we have got attached to the idea that I am the body-mind complex, and it has been the source of our suffering due to the unending wish for many desires that are tied to "I" and "mine."

We need to slowly remove impurities from the mind and understand who we are. This is the practice for all spiritual seekers and for those who want permanent happiness. It is said, "To the one who chooses the Atman, the Atman reveals itself."

Calling ourselves Rita or Sita, John or Paulo is only a reference and a name for the psychophysical being. At the core, the Atmans of Rita and Sita and John and Paulo are the same. One Atman is not distinguishable from another. It is the individual mind that creates the differences in all beings.

Spirit and matter are poles apart from each other: matter is impermanent and changing; spirit is eternal and is timeless, having no beginning and no end. "Whatever is seen is matter, and whatever is matter is un-Atman."[7]

The path of discovering "who am I?" is the critical underpinning for all spiritual evolution.

Understanding who we are was the first major milestone of our journey!

---

[7] Yat drishyam tad jadam, yad jadam tad unatma. (Sanskrit).

The Concept of God

The mighty Atman, essence of our own beings, lies hidden under the layers of our gross bodies and under the subtle bodies of our mind. Our true nature, which is referred to as Atman, is concealed due to lack of knowledge, nothing else. We could, at this very moment, attain enlightenment by living and being who we are. Through a combination of self-effort and divine grace, this understanding will come to be. Spiritual evolvement rests on nothing except the will to evolve. Just as we clean a diamond by removing mud and rock, so too the Atman needs to shine through the filter of our mind. The cleaning agent then is the yoga of knowledge.[8]

There are two truths that are undeniable: we can say with complete conviction that "I am" and that "I know I am." This implies that our awareness is proof of our existence, and it also implies that we are conscious of the fact that we exist. This may sound simplistic, but the implication of such a statement is profound. I am not only aware of myself, but I am aware of all around me—the chair, the new book, my blue sweater, her pet, my house, his daughter, their mansion, the tree in

---

[8] Jnana Yoga (Sanskrit)

my backyard, the seasons, the Swahili language, the absence of horns on a rabbit, the concept of time and space.

It means that consciousness is existence itself. This existence is not merely "is-ness" but is also "*sentient* is-ness." *It has the consciousness principle as its nature. The most ancient wisdom of five to six thousand years ago defines God as Existence-Consciousness-Bliss.*[9] *This is the highest Truth available. It cannot be denied, for we cannot deny ourselves and our experience.*

Due to Consciousness, we are able to move our finger, wiggle our nose, and speak truths and lies. At the individual level, Consciousness is referred to as Atman; however, the spirit exists not only at the level of one being, but all beings.

Every being has a different body and a different mind, but the Spirit, *since it is devoid of any attributes*, is the same in all beings. Spirit is more subtle than the five elements we talked about earlier. It is definitely subtler than earth, water, fire. It is more subtle than air or space. The implication of this subtleness is that it pervades all. Not only is Consciousness in our body, but it also exists between beings, connecting all things in the universe. It pervades all, just as space does. Space can be found between the teeth of a fine comb or between stars in the sky. So too Consciousness is everywhere in the form of existence and awareness. It exists in every speck of the entire universe and beyond.

Once upon a time a young fish came to meet a Guru fish, and asked the question: "Guru-fish, Guru-fish: my father told me that there is water everywhere. But I cannot see it. Please show me where water is?"

In the same way, Consciousness pervades all. Existence is everywhere, whether it manifests itself as a life form or not. With humans, Consciousness manifests itself as existence and awareness; but when

---

[9] Satyam-jnanam-anantam (Sanskrit)

it is matter—for example, a rock, a tree, a carpet, or a fruit—only the existence principle is manifested because a rock is not self-aware.

At the individual or micro level, Consciousness is referred to as Atman; and at the macro level, where it is infinite, the same Consciousness is referred to as Brahman.

Just as space appears finite within a pot and infinite in the universe, so too Atman appears finite in the body but is part of infinity in the universe. Brahman is Existence-Consciousness-Bliss, the Supreme Reality, the One Truth, the Ultimate Reality. It is commonly symbolized as ॐ (Om). One may refer to it as God.

To know that this Consciousness is myself is the highest achievement. Nothing greater can be experienced. It is Me and it is Everything in the universe. Our vision of the world changes because we are no longer divided. Because we are all One, we have no particular attachments and are not bound.

All experiences happen on the base of this One Consciousness. Consciousness is present in all things. The space, the air that connects things is pervaded by the same Consciousness. We are all connected. Experiences come and go but Consciousness always is. People come and go, mountains and planets come and go, but Consciousness always is.

All manifestations, which come in the form of matter, occur on Consciousness, stay awhile, and then dissolve back into the same Consciousness. All change that happens needs a base on which to change. This base is none other than Brahman. It is One Undivided Mass of Unending (spatially), Infinite (time-wise) Consciousness, which is actually beyond both time and space. Time and space are required only for creation. But Consciousness simply Is. It does not have to Become. That is why it is known as Absolute. *The Absolute is the substratum on which relative things (that need space and time) exist.*

In the changing universe, we find all matter changing, but Consciousness does not change. Just as space is one big mass of unending, indivisible matter, Consciousness too is undivided and continuing, eternal and unlimited. You may say space is divided—here I have put a wall between space—but yet, the wall occupies the space as well.

Because it cannot be divided, it cannot be destroyed by any manifested thing. Can space be cut up into pieces, burnt, or beaten to a pulp? Can we destroy space using any weapon, be it a hammer, a sword, or a weapon of mass destruction? No! Even if we break it into parts and try to destroy it, it cannot be. So how can Consciousness, which is a million times more subtle than space, be destroyed?

Consciousness is the epitome of peace. Truth or God does not work under chaos. If you ask why God creates starving children in slums and why a prince is born in a palace, He does not. *He would be a cruel God if such randomness and defects would take place, so we reject the notion of a God that rewards or punishes.* It makes no sense. By definition, God cannot be cruel or partial. Brahman is said to be Pure and Unadulterated.

Just as in the case of the Atman or individual spirit, Brahman is also the source for all happiness. We understand existence and awareness as "I am" and "I know I am", but why should this Existence-Consciousness be the source of blissfulness?

When we talk about happiness, we usually think of pleasure. As discussed earlier, we know we move from activity to activity, trying to gain pleasure. During the downtime between bouts of pleasure, the mind wanders into the past and future: thinking about what happened a while ago or yesterday and what may happen tomorrow. The mind wanders into all directions, causing emotional turmoil, excitement, or upheaval. This can happen while we perform an activity or even when confronted with nothingness.

When we recognize our spiritual being and are immersed in it, we go beyond the mind. It is the mind that is endlessly restless, agitated, frustrated. At the level of the Supreme Truth, we have gone beyond the worldly, material, secular mind.

Just as words are born from silence and move back into silence, so too our mind is born from tranquility and goes back into tranquility.

Beyond the filter of the anxious mind lie Pure Existence, Peace, Infinity, and Perfection. When we experience the Truth directly, after having dissolved the mind and the ego, even for a second, we move closer to spiritual enlightenment. This is Bliss and a state of unchanging, elevated Happiness.

Thus, the Truth, omniscient and omnipotent, is worthy of praise. Only that which is permanent, never changing, and is the source of all things is worthy of worship. Would we ever give a second look to that which is false? Would we ever care for a fake diamond, counterfeit money, hypocritical friend, or an empty promise? The Truth is worshipable because it does not change over time. Things that are changing do not give us a sense of confidence nor can they be a source of strength. They are unreliable and variable. The Truth sets us free because the mind need not entertain hopes and be tangled in anxieties.

Therefore, God, in fact, is Truth, Reality, the Ultimate Reality, the Ultimate Cause, Consciousness-Existence-Bliss (Satyam-Jnanam-Anandam), or any other name you may wish to bestow upon It.

Understanding God as one undivided, continuous, unchanging, blissful, and infinite Consciousness is the second major milestone on our journey!

Universal Laws

The universe has cosmic order.[10] This order is apparent in the laws of nature such as the accuracy of the orbits in the solar system, the rise and fall of tides, the rising and setting of the sun and the moon, the rhythm of a heartbeat, the time for a fetus to evolve, the role of weight and mass upon speed, etc. All these laws are supported by the many sciences of physics, chemistry, biology, mathematics, etc.

Cosmic order is inherent in Brahman. Due to this phenomenon, sages say that *Brahman is Pure Intelligence*. This intelligence, these laws, this order are inherent in the lives of all beings and nonbeings. This intelligence is obviously self-operative and self-governing, meaning that Brahman needs nothing else to tell it what to do or how to do it. It spans the entire visible and invisible cosmos. Even if the whole cosmos becomes unmanifest, the Truth remains. Pure Intelligence remains. Brahman remains.

It is easy to see the physical laws of the universe, but less easy to see more subtle laws.

---

[10] Rtm (Sanskrit)

A subtle law that we can see the manifestation of is gravity. We cannot see this very intelligent principle, but we know of its existence. We can see it in the form of its effect, but we cannot see the cause. We normally ignore subtle laws because we are ignorant of their existence. They are certainly not visible. We take the effects and call them "luck" or "nature."

What subtle laws are these? Remember we operate at two levels: physical and mental. Subtle laws exist at the mental and intellectual level. *At the subtle level, all things also operate through Pure Intelligence. All actions performed sooner or later deliver a result in accordance with the intensity and intent of the action.* In physics, we say everything has an opposite and equal reaction. This is just as true at the nonphysical level. Every effect must have a cause.[11] It cannot be otherwise.

Subtle laws are more pervasive and fine, penetrate deeper and wider than physical laws. Their proof is limited, but by extension of reasoning, we can infer them. An example of a subtle law is an idea. An idea like "capitalism" is more pervasive than a physical law, and the consequences of an idea penetrate deeper and wider. The idea of capitalism is the cause, and one of the effects is the obvious growth in industrialization. Other examples: a subtle cause is insulting someone in childhood, the memory of it when grown-up is the subtle effect. A subtle cause is a smile; the warmth and connection felt is the effect.

It is said that Brahman is the cause, and the world is the effect. The cause, being Pure Intelligence, is one and the effects are many. The whole universe contains names and forms. They include the smallest of things like insects, coal, diamonds, shells, seeds, honeycombs, grains of sand; and they include the largest of things such as oceans, deserts, constellations, suns, moons, stars, galaxies, and the human mind. All these names and forms are the diverse manifestations of the One Intelligence, working in unison as the gigantic wheel of life.

---

[11] Karya kaaran sambandh (Sanskrit).

Universal laws are self-operative and exist without the direct involvement of Consciousness. Let us understand this important principle by using an example. The eyes are unaffected by what they see. They can look at a beautiful flower or a dump of garbage and stay uninvolved. Eyes do not judge, they merely see. In the same way, *Consciousness itself is untouched by the laws, though these very laws exist due to Pure Intelligence. All, then, is subject to cosmic governance.* The sayings "You will reap what you sow" or "What goes around comes around" are very apt!

Thus, the Truth, omnipresent, omniscient, and omnipotent, is very much worthy of praise. And is worshipable. Because the Truth is conscious and intelligent, it is omniscient. Since the Truth is all pervading or omnipresent, covering every nook and cranny of the manifested and unmanifested universe, it knows everything. Because it knows everything, it is omnipotent—meaning it has the knowledge and potential to do anything. Since it is infinite in time and infinite in space, it transgresses the human concepts of time and space.

Any intelligent person understanding this without the demands of his or her personal and limited ego, will stand with awe and wonder at the depth of these revelations of ancient knowledge and wisdom.

Understanding that the Intelligent Brahman works in unison as One Intelligence in the gigantic wheel of life is the third major milestone on our journey!

Maya

The Truth is only One. All else is delusory: delusion because we see things the way we want to see them.

Imagine a young man, Kris, walking into a room where there are twenty people sitting around the table. All attention is, at that moment, drawn to Kris. One lady at the end of the table thinks, "He seems like a nice young man. I would like to get to know him better." Another looks at him and thinks, "He seems to be a little callous, like Uncle Jo. I don't get good vibes." Yet another wishes that the meeting will end quickly but thinks Kris is taking his own sweet time.

Although none of them know the young man, each has judged him, calculated him on the basis of their past experiences. Before Kris has had a chance to speak, all have created an opinion about him. Actually, in the space of ten seconds, all have reacted to him with their body language! Now, the question is who of the twenty is correct?

The answer is that no one actually knows the truth; all is imagined. Even Kris has an opinion about himself! He also cannot be excused from false thinking.

It is not that Kris is false: he is very much present. So is the room and the twenty people in it. Worldly things are not false as such, but the world of the mind superimposes itself on things innocent and neutral. Things just are, but our mind interprets them the way it wants to. *We project our own thoughts on things and people of the world. That is why the rishis say that the world is actually an illusion. This illusion is called Maya. It can be understood as the mind's delusion.*

So if our mind is false, what is the truth? The only truth is that the young man exists. The room exists and the twenty people exist. On further clarification, we cannot even say the room and people exist because my eyes may be faulty. We see one man, the spider sees a hundred men, while the bat sees none. Who is correct? We only see what our eyes allow us to see, and what our ears allow us to hear, etc.

We continuously examine, rationalize, and focus on the world through the constructs of our mind. Because of the way we have judged the world, we have limited our actions. Our constricted actions are usually driven by fear, and unknowingly, we create our own stresses.

If someone has an opinion of us, we do not realize that the opinion that he offers us about ourselves is only through the filter of his or her mind. In actual fact, it is false. What criteria is the person using to judge us? The criteria are questionable, the judgment is questionable, so the actions based on the judgment are questionable.

In the same way, our view of the world is only that: it is questionable.

Seeing neutrality in all things frees us form suffering. When it snows, it is neither good nor bad; it is just snowing. When John gets angry, he is angry not because of you but because of his own mind. When someone ignores you, it is *their* mind not you or your mind that is in question. When we meet someone, they are what they are. When people insult us or have a low opinion of us, it comes from the filter of *their* mind. So too we do the same. *All things, simply put, are what they are. Leave them be without imposition of a particular thought, without making them personal.*

In this world, when we start judging, we end up taking sides. But knowing the mind is conditioned, whose side can we take? To everything, there are two sides of the coin: two opposites. Does the tree give shade to the traveler, or does the tree prevent sunshine for the flowers underneath? Shall we cut the tree because of it? Does the rain help plants grow, or does it dampen the day for us? All is relative: we live in a relative world. Judgment is never absolute.

A question comes to mind: How is it that we have come to be deluded? How is it that we have paid so much attention to a world that is imagined? We take all for granted. We take our own thoughts for granted. We believe ourselves to be right, and then we experience conflicts. We endure others, others endure us. We suffer for it.

If we are the pure Atman and our nature is divine and impeccably pure, how is it that we are stressed and anxious? How can we come home to our pure nature?

The oft-used example of the snake illustrates how we have taken our mind to be so reliable. It illustrates how we have taken for granted the certainness of all things. We believe, undeniably, that our mind's thinking is indisputable. The example is this: Imagine walking into a room with very dim lighting. Suddenly, you see a long thin curvy object on the floor. You jump at the sight of the snake and take a step back. You are afraid and about to flee the scene when you quickly switch on the flashlight and immediately realize that it is a rope and not a snake. You give a huge sigh of relief.

The snake that was initially seen is not true—it was an illusion. The rope was thought to be a snake. This illusion that it was a snake was located in our mind. When the rope, through the mind, appeared as a snake, it did not actually turn into a snake; in ignorance, we assumed incorrectly. When knowledge dawned on us that the snake was really a rope, we realized our mistake. The fear and insecurity created were merely an illusion.

In the same way, in spiritual realization, we come to know that our mind is deluded. The mind is false although we assume that our thoughts are true. When we get caught up with the world, all that we see around us is assumed to be true, not false. Just as the snake is mentally imposed on the rope due to imagination, *the world is imagined in our mind.* In the example of the young man, Kris, there were twenty imagined worlds in the room, each significantly different from the other.

Next time you sit around the table for a meal with friends or family, imagine the world inside each one's mind. How different each one is from the other. The world inside our heads is so unique that no one can possibly know exactly what the other world feels like. How differently it is that we view things, approach things, think, and react. It is amazing that we can even communicate with one another and make ourselves understood. That is why we often say, "No one understands me."

We have seen falseness of the world from a psychological perspective. Another aspect looks at the physical side of falseness.

Anything we see today is *deemed* to be true. When we see the sky and water as blue, it is false although we assume it to be true. Neither air nor water are blue; they are transparent. They are only *apparently* blue. The sun is *apparently* setting. The rain is innocent, but it is *apparently* a menace. We see and sense the world through our limited and distorted senses. One needs eyeglasses to correct vision. If a person does not have corrective glasses, he does not know that what he sees is false. In the same way, we mistakenly see the world through our limited senses and mind and assume that to be true.

Let us continue with the physical perspective of delusion. We see an apple today. The apple is only true in the present. Yesterday, it was a mere seed; and tomorrow, it will rot and fall to the ground. We can only call an apple an apple at the present moment. All things in the universe come with a form. We give this form a name simply for utilitarian value. We keep giving new forms new names, e.g., PCs, iPods, satellites, Highway 417. We have a utilitarian view of all things. But in actual fact all is impermanent. A piece of paper, for example, is only a piece of paper at this point in time. Yesterday it was a tree, and tomorrow it will be ashes. The mind interprets all through the lens of our present conditioning. Taking the physical world for granted gives us a narrow focus and creates suffering and sorrow. After all, we ourselves never expect our own bodies to die! We expect permanency in all things.

In spiritual evolution, we see that there are two types of illusions: One is that of seeing something physically as false, like the setting sun; and two, seeing the world through our mind, which is conditioned. Both are limiting, and therefore, the causes of fear and unhappiness.

In the example of the rope and the snake, the snake was superimposed on the rope. In the same way, the illusory world is superimposed on the Ultimate Reality. Without the support of this Reality, nothing is. The fact that the paper is a tree, the tree was manifested due to the potential that was in a seed, etc., shows that existence is, but in different forms. If we take away all that is manifested, only Reality will remain. In fact, only a very minute portion of the world is manifested, and only part of that manifestation is available through our senses.

Seeing the world in its totality frees the mind. It takes us away from the mundane. It releases us from constraints of the mind and empties the mind of all limitations. The empty mind can then start to focus on the Truth, on the Largeness of Life.

When we see the Everest from the south, we are looking at it from one angle. When we see it from China or Tibet, it takes on different dimensions. Only when we stand on the peak of the Everest itself, all becomes visible. There are no more angles; we can see all. So too, with spiritual evolution, we see All.

Impermanence of the world makes us realize the frailty and smallness of the world. We do not even live long enough to see trees and mountains perish. All manifestations come and go. Even planets and stars come and go; what of cars and roads and gas stations, tables and chairs, stocks, and trends, and ideas? What of people around us?

In the scheme of things, who and what are we? Only a speck in this mighty universe with extremely limited experiences. Yet we take everything so seriously and suffer the consequences!

Maya is that which makes the false appear true. Understanding that the delusory power of Maya takes us away from Truth and Permanent Happiness, and does not allow us to experience who we really are is the fourth major milestone in our spiritual journey.

Desires

At the very root of the minds' restlessness, agitation, and frustration is desire. Not being able to fulfill one's desires causes great unhappiness.

I can shop but not find the outfit I am looking for. For me to be pleased, it must be the right fit, the right color, the right look. If Baskin Robbins does not carry my favorite flavor, I am disappointed. If I do not see my best friend at the party, I am disappointed. If Cantonese noodles are not on the menu, I am disappointed. If I do not get my promotion, I am disappointed. If my spouse does not get me flowers, I am disappointed. There are so many things I want; the list is never ending.

Desires are of many kinds:[12] desire for name and fame, desire for power, desire for money, desire for knowledge, desire for sensuous pleasures, desire for children are just a few. There are big things in life we want, and there are little things in life we want.

---

[12] Lokeshna, Vittesna, Putreshna (Sanskrit)

Desire for basic living is not included here: food and shelter are fundamental needs. They are natural and required. What is meant by desire is the incessant yearning for specific things, which result in my feeling "happy." We set our hearts on many things: it could be a car, a relationship, or a vacation. Sometimes our desires are more subtle. We may want certain gestures of love or acceptance or praise and recognition from our loved ones, from our parents, or our bosses. We can have desires to achieve a particular goal in life like being the best musician or owning our own business or getting married and having a family.

When desires are not realized, we feel disappointed and unfulfilled. They nag at us, and we pursue them until we are able to get what we want or until we have depleted our energies. Either curbing our desires or fulfilling them seems to be the only two ways to achieving happiness. The rishis claim that the fewer desires we have, the happier we will be. If there are minimal expectations of the world we live in, anything coming our way will be a newfound joy.

So what is the answer? Should we have no desires at all? Should we not have any goals or ambitions? Should we become dry and stoic?

Wisdom says two things: (1) that we should aim to fulfill the desire itself but not entertain the desire for the "fruits of action" and (2) that we invite trouble when the mind insists on a very particular outcome.

Take a student who is studying for his exam. When the examination is being written, the student must focus his energy on writing, not on the result. Concentration on the outcome would only serve to distract the student, making his chance of success worse. Also, accepting this kind of a philosophy eases the burden on self-expectations, and the resulting self-worth.

Let us suppose we are unemployed and looking for a job. The desire to land a job is reasonable and expected. We should do all that is necessary to fulfill this need, but since the outcome is not directly in our hands, we should let go once the ball is rolling. Understand that the result is beyond your control. What is unreasonable for us is to insist that we will only be happy if we get *that* job, doing *that* type of work under only *those* conditions. Thinking in that way, we lock ourselves into a corner. Even though we have opportunities for interviews and possibilities of working, we feel dissatisfied unless we obtain exactly what we want. Often I will hear people resort to verbiage like "Oh, don't get me wrong, I *like* it but . . ." and "It's okay for now, I guess" or "I was looking for a red one but they didn't have any, so I settled for this green one." In these cases, we have insisted on a very particular outcome. Again, to have desires is natural, but to insist on a particular outcome is disaster.

There is a severe and subtle chain reaction that we need to be cognizant of with unfulfilled desires. They cause anger and frustration in us. In our moment of anger, we lose perspective and clarity of the goal; and instead of sitting back and reevaluating the situation from a larger perspective and dealing with the issue constructively, we react by blaming, shouting, withdrawing, etc. Anger distorts our vision and causes delusional or unclear thinking. It makes us react through habitual patterns; and if we are prone to anxiety, stress, or depression, we feel defeated and devastated. It seems that there is no answer, that no one is on our side, and no one understands us.

Anger takes many forms, which create negative tendencies in the mind. If I entertain a desire and it is not fulfilled, I get angry at the person or object obstructing my desire. If someone *else* gets what *I* want, anger turns into jealousy. If I fulfill my desire and have actually "won" it over someone else, I gloat and develop pride. If I cannot get my desire at all, I hate the circumstances and those responsible for my circumstances. If I get what I want, I become greedy and want more.

Negative thoughts are a result of desire: fulfilled or unfulfilled.

There is no end to desire. It consumes all our efforts and our energy. It wants more and more until we are thrown from one side to another, thrashed by its insatiability. Even then we do not stop. It is said that our hairs will turn grey and there will be no teeth left, but the force of desire will never cease.

Desires also compromise our well-being by promoting one obsession at the expense of another. For example, we purchase a car at the expense of being financially insecure; we eat ice cream at the expense of our health. For a more subtle example, we may choose to stay in an unhealthy relationship at the expense of our freedom; we may wish to pursue our career at the expense of our family obligations. We are faced with difficult situations because in most cases we do not expect to give up anything to obtain something new, yet in most cases, we have to make some kind of a sacrifice. In the case of objects and material possessions, this concept is easy to understand; but the difficult choices are usually more subtle. They make us choose between what we long for versus what is good for us. This creates inner conflict.

It is absurd and illogical to think that the pursuit of personal desires will bring us happiness in the long run. How can we be happy at the cost of compromising ourselves? We give up long-term gain for short-term satisfaction, forgetting that thinking long term actually increases our chances of sustained happiness.

Conflict and compromise promote stress and depression. On the one hand, we are not happy if we chose sensibility over pleasure; and on the other, we suffer the consequences of pursuing pleasure.

The stronger our desire is, the more vulnerable we become. Unless our character is grounded, we take shortcuts to reach our goal as quickly as possible. It is why people shoplift or do not give back the correct change. These are small examples, but they are the small wrongdoings that plant the mental seeds for cases like Enron, which have at its root nothing but selfish greed and desire.

Desire for name, fame, and power are the hardest desires to overcome. We see political agendas at organizations, corporations, or businesses, e.g., taking credit when it is not due, suppressing talents and threats, protecting turf and territory for financial security and for retaining power. Empires are generally built on selfish ambition. It is because of these vasanas (tendencies) that destructive politics, exploitation, and oppression run rampant. The undercurrent of conflict spreads and war is justified. Mahatma Gandhi, the great leader who wanted nothing for himself, said, "Earth provides enough to satisfy every man's need, but not every man's greed."

Desires, on the other hand, that are well intentioned and selfless, do not compromise our sense of duties. Although they require patience and strength, they are healthier in the long run. Selfless desires need to be nurtured, for example, listening to music, cooking for oneself and others, spending time with family and friends, sharing moments and thoughts. The path to enlightenment is lit up with elevated thoughts and sentiments.

Now, the question may arise, and people will ask, "If we don't have any desires, how can we achieve anything at all? Am I not supposed to have any ambition or a future? How will I ever be successful and happy if I don't work towards what I want?"

Of course, one must have goals and plans to secure a future. However, to insist on a very specific and defined outcome can create stress, anger, and aggravation. Focus is good, but expectation and insistence of a precise result is disaster.

The way to balance desires and expectations is by simply charting a general direction. Then, we accept things as they unfold, making our small choices as we go along. We cannot control the big things in life, only little ones. Get things in motion and let it be. Insisting on a particular fruit of action and expecting it to happen the way we want it to is itself an unreasonable desire!

The laws of the universe will work themselves out as they are supposed to. Every cause in the universe will have its own effects. At the aggregate levels of the world, the laws will govern order; and at the individual level too, our own previous causes will create their effects.

In spiritual evolvement, Happiness is contingent upon effortlessly letting go of the "fruits of our desires."

Karma

The word "karma" comes from the word "karm" in Sanskrit, "to act" or "to do." It is quite obvious that one cannot live in the world without performing an action or doing something; it is what experiences are made of. Although certain behaviors elicit certain results, expected outcomes may or may not happen. Even a child knows that "being good or bad" will ensure Santa's presents. But when expectations do not correspond to our actions, we wonder what happened.

This law, though extremely subtle and sophisticated, is entrenched in cosmic order. It is one of the reasons why all religions give importance to the golden rule "As you sow, so shall you reap." At the physical level, this cause-effect relationship is easy to observe. For example, if I eat fifty thousand calories a day without working it off, I will gain weight; if I do not get ready on time, I will be late for my appointment.

At the finer level, doing a good deed for someone will be remembered. Insulting or admiring someone, getting angry, or insulting someone will be remembered. When these events happen, a series of subtle consequences are set in motion. There are psychophysical repercussions, and resulting impressions are accumulated as merits and demerits.

For example, supposing we met someone at a party and got into an argument, the consequence may be that we will not want to interact with them again. Or we may want to settle the score next time we meet them. Either of these two actions will create ongoing consequences and impressions in the form of negative thoughts. Many choices are open to us in this example: we may insult them or hold a long-term grudge against them, we may ignore them or talk behind their back. All different actions are possible. The point is that there will definitely be a consequence from the initial behavior whether it is good or bad, right or wrong, respectful or impertinent, appropriate or improper, acceptable or offensive.

Consequences can be immediate or take years to manifest.

Man has free will and man can exercise that free will. Man is different than an animal because an animal lives by mechanical instinct. Men have choices to make: we can make good choices or bad choices. *But also, man has the power to decide if he wants to make good choices only.* We are all responsible for our actions. Karma should be thought of less as a moral discipline and more as a spiritual direction.

We create our own outcomes with every word we utter, every gesture, every thought, every deed we perform. The smallest decision will have a consequence. The law of karma dictates that every action will have an equal consequence, now or later.

This is how we make our own destiny.

It is not the actual act that creates karma, but the motive with which it is done. Obviously, the same act can be performed for different reasons. We may throw the monkey in the zoo peanuts because we want to feed him, or we may throw the monkey nuts because we want to tease him. In either case, the act of throwing peanuts is the same but the intention is different. We may phone Aunt Ethel to wish her Merry Christmas or we may phone Aunt Ethel to secretly ensure we get a Christmas present. The act of phoning Aunt Ethel is the same in both cases but the intention is different. The intent of a doctor plunging a knife in a body is different than that of a murderer plunging a knife in a body. So the intent is what matters, not the act itself.

Karma spans across time, and the effects of karma meet us sometime in the future. Some of the karmic impressions that we formed earlier create the present, and other results have yet to be fructified.

A consequence may not be immediate but will definitely follow. Eating polluted foods will cause health issues later in life, denials in childhood will create psychological disturbances later in life, untreated teeth will develop cavities, a mechanical defect during the construction of an airplane will cause disaster later. Failure to uphold responsibilities in life will produce undesired results, which in time will affect relationships. Inspirations from good role models will naturally instigate noble and lofty thoughts later. Association with positive people will bolster positive energy, and conversely, staying in a negative environment will undermine positive growth.

Effects from past actions are being experienced today. This is referred to as *prarabdha* or destiny. Not only our physical but our psychological state is due to our past actions. You may say that the past is one factor affecting my situation, but sometimes I have no control over what is happening in my life: I am forced to take a certain action because a curve is thrown at me. True, things happen to us without us causing them directly, but the cosmic laws of the universe have already started dictating their effects from past actions. Whatever is experienced today is an effect of yesterday. There are no exceptions. One cannot get away from the law of gravity or any other laws in the physical universe. In the same way, one cannot escape the workings of the subtle laws.

Our birth, our parents, our circumstances, our health, our economic standing are the big karmic consequences that we have no control over. Of course, universal laws bring other factors into consideration. Sometimes situations are created to make us choose the right path. The situation may be unpleasant but it is the learning from it that is important. This is free will at work. Sometimes there is no time to think and we need to react instantly. This is where consistent practice of right choices will help us move in the right direction by default.

Self-effort in making right choices is known as *purushartha*. Making full effort to counteract negative effects of karma is captured in later chapters that deal with values and dharma.

Sometimes you will be good to one person but he or she may not reciprocate. It is not necessary that the good result will come back from that *very same* person. In the gigantic wheel of life, you may receive the deserved goodness from somewhere else, but it is guaranteed that you will receive goodness for your good deed. One should earn merit, it will prove more useful than earning wealth.

Having said that karma is responsible for our present condition does not mean that we judge people by their social standing, their health, or wealth. Judging them in this way creates negative karma for the thinker. Remember, we can at anytime be in the shoes of another due to Karma that has not yet been activated—in this life or the next. If we keep that thought top of mind, our arrogance will be weakened.

What we do in life and the choices we make in our lives right now are responsible for creating the future. Freedom of choice is a privilege that we have, that we must exercise with alertness.

Understanding karma and its effects is the fifth major step towards our spiritual journey.

Reincarnation

Death is inevitable for all. Death, in spirituality, is the disassociation of the subtle body from the physical body, and reincarnation is the returning of the subtle body in a new physical being. The subtle body holds in it all the skills, talents, ideas, tendencies, propensities, personalities, yearnings, impressions in a latent form. We never lose our knowledge, our talents, our wisdom, or our merits and demerits across life spans.

What is the proof of reincarnation? Why does half the world believe in this phenomenon? What is the proof of an afterlife—of heaven and hell? Or of any other afterlife? Most religions believe in the afterlife and believe in the immortal soul. We should remember, very importantly, that while we cannot prove this phenomenon conclusively, we also cannot disprove it.

Logic dictates that if cosmic order is present, then people cannot be born willy-nilly and unfairly. One cannot be born under better circumstances than another for no apparent reason. To believe that is illogical. To believe that by luck one has a better or worse standing in life makes little sense. If we say, "Oh, it is due to random nature," we must necessarily be believing in some kind of magic: by magic I was born here; by magic, food will be cooked on its own; by magic, this woman will become the president of a country; by magic, my child will be intelligent and handsome!

Magic implies no effort or order. This is absurd thinking, especially for the scientific brains that we claim to have in this twenty-first century! Cosmic laws will make no sense if our labor of love is unfulfilled, if criminals go without retribution, if there are no consequences of actions.

The theory of reincarnation is based upon the continuance of karma. Just as we perform actions during the day, go to sleep that night, and reap the consequences of what we ate last night the next morning, we reap the consequences of this life in the next. It is the same logic extended further. The law does not come to an abrupt stop the minute the physical body dies. With the demise of the physical body, the subtle aspects still remain. Let us take a car on the highway for example. You are driving from Toronto to Montreal, and suddenly the car spurts and comes to a halt. When we realize that the reason the car failed is because of a depleted gas tank, the car must eventually start from where it left off. *In the same way, when one dies, one starts the next life from where one left off.* The subtle characteristics and personalities of a person continue on as if they never left.

Each life builds on the previous. Just as a relationship is built on all previous experiences, our life is built on previous lives. *All our impressions in this life will be accumulated on a rolling basis and added to the next one. All unfulfilled desires in this life will be carried on to the next.* Our samskaras and vasanas will be kept intact and taken into the future life. Any good or bad karma also stays intact and is taken into the new life. It is illogical to say that there are no consequences of actions performed, that when the physical structure departs, nothing remains. Even when water evaporates, it continues to exist in the subtle form. When saints die, their ideas exist; when corporations die, their repercussions continue. When thoughts and events conclude, their impressions stay. The subtle always outlives the gross. Even chocolate, after consumption, leaves a subtle aftertaste; a light, when turned off, takes seconds to go away. A PC, after shutting down, takes a few more moments to come to a complete halt, and a fan takes time to stop rotating after it is switched off. The subtle outlives the gross, so too our bodies.

So what is that which is reborn we may ask? The subtle body that remains includes our mind, intellect, vasanas, impressions, tendencies, and the "aftertaste" of any memories. It is why we are born with personalities. Even small children have their very own personalities.

In one house, many children are born, yet they may have significantly different personalities, talents, skills, aptitudes, abilities, and natures. This is due to the accumulation of experiences in previous lives. *Everyone brings with them the fragrance of all their past lives, which are countless in number.*

Now the question that arises in one's mind is how many lives have I lived and will this go on eternally? What is it that makes me be born again and again?

Let us take our ordinary lives and use that to develop our thought.

In the course of a day, I may want to do several things. When I wake up in the morning, my mind gets flooded by things I need to do: I need to wash up, I need to eat breakfast, drive to work, attend to meetings and customers, come back home, go to the gym, call my doctor for an appointment, make a dinner reservation for next week, prepare dinner, pack lunch for tomorrow, and go to bed. If I cannot get all that done in one day, I will postpone some things for the next day. Perhaps taking the doctors appointment is not an immediate priority; it can be done later. Perhaps the desire to cook something did not transpire today due to lack of time, and it is postponed to the future.

Now, during the day, new demands will arise—I may need to help my mother or visit a sick friend or prepare a presentation, and I will need to add these new items to the original "to do" list.

In one life too, we have many plans and desires that we want to fulfill. And along the course of life, new ideas and desires get added and replaced constantly. We are quite unaware of the change in our psychological state as time passes. It is something we do not pay attention to. We are very cognizant of the changes in the physical body but not so at the more subtle level of the mind. All these old and new desires put together will take more than a lifetime to fulfill. Just as we tend to priority items in one day, so too, we prioritize the activities in one's life.

Based on the intensity of desire, we accumulate lives with things to accomplish and experience. Most of our desires are impossible to fill in one lifetime, and unknowingly, we have planned many more lifetimes ahead of us. In actual fact, all our desires have a very good chance of getting fulfilled simply because we want them. Conflicting desires such as being Mother Teresa *and* being a millionaire cannot be fulfilled in one lifetime. They create "reincarnation longevity." *Karma and reincarnation are based on a continuous chain of pursuing and fulfilling desires.*

We need to question where this continuous need for fulfilling our desires gets us. Does it give us the happiness we are seeking? If we keep completing one desire after another, are we in fact getting happier with each life?

Economic achievement or any other self-serving achievement in itself serves only the purpose of pampering ourselves. We fill our lives with temporary enjoyments. We have been happy in many instances of our life, but they are forgotten today, having been replaced by new goals and new aspirations. We are now working very hard to fulfill the new set of objectives that were quite nonexistent five, ten, or twenty years ago.

The goal of all lives, unquestionably, is to reach a state of *sustained* happiness; and ultimately, we crave total and unending fulfillment. This fulfillment can only be achieved when we liberate ourselves from all bondage. This is technically called moksha and is commonly known as enlightenment.

When enlightenment occurs, all desires are fulfilled all at once. And reincarnation comes to a stop. Then, if one holds infinity in the palm of one's hand, of what use is grasping the many finite desires?

Good and Bad

Controlling the mind, as we know, is a challenge which many of us cannot successfully manage. But what does it mean? How and what do we want to control? The quantity and quality of thoughts? What kind of thoughts? The mind needs to make right choices. What are right choices?

Cultivating and developing the mind needs more clarity. When we are young, we do not have the ability to distinguish what is good for us and what will create problems. As children, we eat what we like, go where we want, say whatever comes to us. It is not until later that we come to be mature and are able to separate some goods and bads. More often than not, we ourselves get mixed up in our understanding of right or wrong, good and bad, should I or shouldn't I? What is attractive is not necessarily good for us, and what seems to need too much patience is too difficult a path for us.

When we let go the reigns of the mind, it easily slips into self-seeking behavior. The mind does not know good from bad unless it has been taught to. Societies have different norms which become part of our conditioning. Except for extreme good and extreme bad, it is hard to differentiate right from wrong.

If we understand intellectually that the mind keeps no restraints on itself, then we have understood the need for values and ideals. Without restraint, we slowly provoke the qualities of disrespect, lack of concern, lust, greed, passion, possession, etc.

Role models in life offer us the values and idealism we aspire to. We admire heroes, saints, women and men in history because of the way they thought and lived. When have we ever admired people for what they possessed materially? Even if we did, it is their courage and intellectual ability to be an entrepreneur that we admire.

The mind needs to associate itself with spiritual values for it to feel truly elevated and fulfilled. These noble values embrace qualities we seek in others, regardless of whether we ourselves have them of not. We value compassion, kindness, thoughtfulness, truth, sincerity, and more from others and admire those who truly have them.

The mind can be nurtured to become placid and serene through vigilant training. The mind needs to be trained with infinite patience. Like a child, we need to treat the mind gently and make it unlearn its old habits and tendencies. If we use strict discipline, we will have the mind's anarchy on our hands! We think it is hard to change others, but try forcing something on ourselves! No wonder it is so hard to diet and keep New Year's resolutions! That is why ancient wisdom touts discipline as a virtue.

Moral and ethical dilemmas can only be resolved through the understanding of values. If we believe that materialism is delightful and charming, safe and secure, and that moral values are dull and boring, then we cannot proceed.

The use of power needs right understanding. Usage of that power, whether you are the breadwinner, whether you are intellectually superior, or whether you are in a high position needs to be accompanied by the virtue of universal justice. After all, the constitution also says every person has the right to pursue liberty and happiness.

For us to embrace values, we must believe in virtues. We must believe that values and virtues are the road to freedom and happiness. And peace, love, and fulfillment must be truly desired over sorrow, discontentment, and fear.

I do not believe that peace and love are devoid of adventure, excitement, and gumption. After all, we are talking about fearlessness and freedom! It is possible to have fun and boldly tread the path of spirituality! It is the challenge and adventure of a lifetime where nothing is required except courage.

Values

The underpinning for happiness lies in good human values. Happiness brought on by material and technological success alone is not wholesome or fulfilling. Unless economic advancement is directed and cushioned by values, we can expect to live in a ruthless, self-centered, and callous society.

To counteract the effects of past karma and ensure a kind future, much attention needs to be paid to human values. This is the self-effort we must put forward.

It is not true that we do not have values but that values have changed over time. Good and moral values determine and uphold the decency, dignity, integrity, and ultimately the happiness of a cultured society. Evolution and progress of any civilization cannot be achieved without values as a basic foundation. Values have changed over time such that value for material gain is held superior to any other values, including moral ones.

Capitalism has forced individuals to compete, dominate, acquire, manipulate and control. Words like rat race, cut-throat competition, drive, undercut, acquire has created a frenzy. Sports analogies dominate the corporate world, and power is deemed a prized possession whether exercised in the office, at home, in the community, or in a political party. Today's emphasis on winning, efficiency, productivity, and economic gain has gone beyond being sensible and reasonable to a new level of self-gratification—the root of which is personal power and the need for glutinous living.

Let us understand that any unit, like a family, a business, or a corporation cannot survive when power-oriented values start to rip the very fiber of the entity. So from the start, competitiveness must be uncompromisingly accompanied and cushioned by more fundamental beliefs and thoughts such as fairness, integrity, trust, etc. Many times, these softer values obstruct unfulfilled, obsessive ambition.

We need to question whether "winning" is bringing with it the happiness we seek as individuals. Is economic and worldly happiness giving us fulfillment?

If individuals in the society are not happy, how can society itself be happy? A nation and the world are built on society and individuals.

Man cannot imbibe both of these sets of values—let us call them power-oriented values versus humanitarian values—at the same time. Such expectations create disharmony in the psyche of individuals. One cannot embrace virtues like fairness, truthfulness, sincerity, integrity, humility in a given setting and then practice manipulation, domination, pretence, self-glorification, favouritism, etc., in another setting.

The internal disharmony itself will create confusion, fear, resentment, and hostility. Power-oriented values innately have the seeds of jealousy, envy, passion, possession, anger, and other destructive tendencies. How can one have a loving family; a gentle, trusted circle of friends; a support network; or an emotional connection under these circumstances?

It is the responsibility of all of us, especially those already in positions of power, to break down this polar structure of current-day values. They need to be harmonized internally within oneself and externally with the outer world.

A beautiful and ancient concept of "dharma" can help us reach the goal of humanitarian values and thus move us towards harmony and happiness.

Dharma

In the spiritual and societal context, the word "dharma" embraces all aspects of personal virtues, which are required for wholesome living.

Dharma is not one word but a way of living. *Dharma is that which supports the entire universe, where each entity supports the existence of itself in its own true nature and that of others in their own true nature.* It encompasses a natural inclination for living conscientiously towards oneself and society; and embeds an attitude of selflessness, integrity, self-awareness, sincerity, and being true to one's own talents and abilities.

Following dharma, the right way of living, has a most awesome reward. Contrary to what you might think, thereafter, one is able to live life relatively stress free. Following dharmic principles alleviates mental stress because we know that there are no negative repercussions of good, healthy, responsible living. Life becomes straightforward and doubtless. Confusions come to an end. Integrity and character are built-up along the path, and respect for all is embedded in thought and behavior.

Although every decade and every culture has its own characteristic values, certain virtues are universal and timeless. To be virtuous is to be good. Why does being good set us free? If we do not have virtuous thoughts, it is obvious that they have been replaced by impure thoughts. If we lack integrity, how can we expect others to trust us? If we are not genuine or sincere, how can anyone believe us? If we are not consistent in our behavior, how can we expect anyone to depend on us? If we cheat, lie, manipulate, or pretend, how can we be valued, appreciated, or respected? If we lack courage, how can we live by our convictions? We need humility, for we can never satisfy our pride and ego. If we lack fairness, no one will trust us or value our judgment or advice. Having negative tendencies may serve us in gaining temporary materialism, but in the longer run, a person never wins. It is said, "Satyam Eva Jayate" or "Only Truth is victorious" because truth, in the widest sense of the term, outlasts all.

The main ingredients for living a dharmic life is living "truthfully" and upholding one's responsibilities.[13] Living truthfully has a wide implication: it encompasses such things as being true to oneself, sharing the burdens of living in a family, being fair and honest, not hurting other living things, speaking the truth, avoiding personal agendas, not taking advantage of others, and not living hypocritically. Living truthfully is a psychological state.

Ancient wisdom clarifies four objectives for mankind:

1. Responsible living (Dharma)

2. Obtaining "wealth" (Artha)

3. Enjoying the earned wealth (Kama)

4. Overcoming worldly living through liberation (Moksha).

Obtaining wealth and enjoying that wealth are the means by which we function in the world. They are both activity based. While Artha

---

[13] Satyam vada, Dharmam chara (Sanskrit).

refers to all forms of worldly wealth and Kama is the enjoyment of that wealth, they both need to be performed on the foundation of dharma—responsible living towards oneself and society. Moksha is the desired state of happiness one reaches when absolute freedom descends in the heart and mind. *In other words, wealth and pleasure should be upheld through correct conduct and ultimately end in complete freedom from any bondage.*

Dharma is not an end in itself. When people think that it is good enough to be a good person, it is not so. We may do good but not be good.

One always has responsibilities towards oneself as much as towards others. Nonviolence to your own self is just as important as nonviolence to others. When we talk about goodness, it is *very* important to note that we should treat ourselves the way we would treat a best friend. Many a time we sacrifice our own happiness and well-being for others, and feel that making sacrifices and being tolerant is inwardly heroic. However, there is a fine line between toleration and self-respect. If we are in an oppressive or submissive situation, we must gain inner strength to uphold dharma for ourselves. This strength is gained by respecting our own freedom and standing up firmly for it. God made all people equal. You are no less than anyone else.

When one does what one is supposed to do, all confusions come to an end. There is no question about making wrong choices since all choices will be founded on virtuous ground. When the ego stops demanding results, personal desires disintegrate and peace enters the heart.

There is a great difference between wanting economic gain and the path to obtaining it. It is the "how" we are addressing, not the "where" we want to reach. We could have the desire to be a millionaire, but how to achieve that wealth and what to do with it are totally different things. *If we are able to have our gains supported by wisdom, tempered by the greater good, then character has no option but to emerge.* Inner strength is derived from conducting oneself impeccably. This takes constant awareness. Worthiness and courage enthuse living. Universal or impersonal love are given and received freely.

Following dharmic principles is the sixth major milestone in our spiritual journey.

Meditation

Meditation is an integral practice in spirituality, which culminates in meditative living. This practice of meditation is necessary for all spiritual seekers because it helps the mind to become more subtle. To grasp the abstract concepts of spirituality, a calm, attentive, uncluttered, subtle mind is required.

Meditation[14] is the means by which the body and the mind become composed. Both the physical and the mental energies need to be reigned in and diffused.

The process requires us first to prepare our sense organs, since they are responsible for bringing distractions from the external world. It is said that we should meditate in a quiet, secluded place, which is clean and pure. There we must sit in a comfortable posture with the head, neck, and spine in a straight line. The best time to meditate is early morning before the mind has had a chance to get into gear.

The next step is to prepare the mind by taking on an attitude of detachment and embracing an attitude of humility, faith, and devotion

---

[14] Dhyana (Sanskrit)

to the desired God or Guru. The reason for doing this is to drop the ego. Unless the "I-ness" is forced out, it is not possible to calm the mind. The "I-and-my" force is a disruptive nuisance that has its own agenda.

With both of these physical and mental preparations completed, we should then begin to withdraw, refraining and restraining our sense organs and our mind. At this point, concentration is necessary. Developing concentration helps the mind become sharp and disciplined. For any activity, even in the secular realm, this concentrated focus is required whether we play the piano, work on an assembly line, or perform surgery. In the spiritual field, the act of meditating is required for slowly bringing the mind to stillness and ultimately to silence.

There are many techniques for meditation. One can chant a desired mantra, gaze at a specific spot, be guided by the tender words of a guru, say a prayer continuously, be inspired using a beautiful verse, observe our own breathing, observe our thoughts as they come, turn the beads of a rosary, or simply read a holy scripture. There are almost as many ways to meditate as there are people. There is no right or wrong way. As long as there is spiritual growth and evolvement due to meditation, one can say that the act of meditating is helping.

My own personal experience has been that it is the change in attitude that is far more effective than any kind of physical concentration. The way to change one's attitude is to understand intellectually the concepts of Vedanta, which provide many of the answers that trouble the mind. Once the mind is satisfied, calmness follows automatically.

Ancient wisdom expounds the processes[15] of listening, analysing and experiencing that one should employ. First, listen to what the philosophy teaches. Then, through reasoning and logic, validate the teachings, and finally "own" and personalize the teachings through your own experiences.

---

[15] Processes of shruti, yukti, and anubhuti (Sanskrit).

Meditation is not the culmination of spirituality; it is a means. In addition, meditation is only one spiritual practice. There are other accompanying preparations that one can undertake in order to evolve beautifully and completely and reach the goal of happiness and freedom.

Meditative Living

Meditative living is a natural result of gaining spiritual knowledge and of spiritual practices.

The word meditation is usually referred to as an act. "To meditate" is an activity, which is time bound. It has a start and an end. This concept of "one hour" meditation is far removed from what the sages intended, though it is essential for starters.

Meditation happens naturally when the conditioning of the mind drops away and pure living becomes spontaneous. It is when we can transcend the mind and lose the ego. The experiencer, the experienced, and the act of experiencing all merge into one. This is a 7*24 state, not an hour-long activity. Ultimately, meditation is living in awareness: a natural awareness of the presence of the Higher Reality. It is not forced; rather, it arrives in the form of graceful living.

The processes that take place to reach this beautiful way of life are varied; however, the primary requirement is discriminative knowledge: the ability to realize the difference between Truth and untruth. We gain clarity of many confusing issues such as who we are and who we are not, how our mind is held bondage to previous conditioning, that karma exists, the laws of the Universe exist, etc.

When knowledge is understood, we move away from the mundane to the higher road of consciousness. The practice of spirituality embraces this new way of thinking, this new attitude. For example, if someone insults us, directly or indirectly, we end up thinking "that person is insulting us based on the condition of *his* mind. That is how he has been taught to think. It has actually nothing to do with me." If someone gets promoted ahead of us or makes more money in business, we can say, "That is the way karma has worked out for him. Let me make use of this opportunity to obtain greater detachment." Still, a more mature mind will accept that it is not the doing of any one individual but the total effect of the cosmic laws. I will do my part. I will do my best, and leave the rest.

With acceptance comes a great fearlessness. We can let go of our anxieties about the future and start to live in the present. In acceptance, there is the humility of not knowing what will happen and an understanding that the Cosmic Intelligence is larger than oneself. If Cosmic Intelligence is self-operative, then one can have full faith that what happens, happens due to various reasons. Remember that there are many causes in the phenomenal world with many effects.

When there is total acceptance, it is called faith. This kind of faith, based on knowledge and understanding, brings a most beautiful relationship between you and the world. *The small "i" goes hand in hand with the big "I" of Consciousness.* We become grateful for the chance we have been given through some mysterious divine grace. Surrender arrives. Fear disintegrates. All things become sacred and the head bows itself in reverence at the Largeness of Life.

Whenever this understanding takes place, we get inspired into action. We cannot help but share. Like a ripe fruit that must fall from the tree, we too, are compelled to share the beautiful move towards liberated living.

Many hours of solitude and reflection, experimentation and reasoning will happen, guiding our interactions, building intuition, and grounding us further into ourselves.

Integrity and great character will emerge from this firmness and faith in Truth. Tenderness, compassion, innocence will reside simultaneously with courage, conviction, and fearlessness. Always standing firm in the understanding of Totality is meditation.

Contrary to popular belief, detachment[16] is not the end-all of spiritual living. On the contrary, detachment should blossom into embracing of the world and its treasures. All are One, One is All.

This is when we will start to live meditatively, bringing together wholesomeness and a total freedom from bondage. Universal love will naturally emanate for all beings and things.

In the process of our development, much attention needs to be paid to our spiritual ego. The spiritual ego is the "i" in us saying, "Look how spiritual I am" (implying, of course, that you are not and therefore I am superior to you). The rise of the spiritual ego is the end of spiritual living. This subtle ego can drive us back into desire for name, fame, and power. People praise, egos grow. The constant reminder in the Largeness of Life and devotion to the Gods and Gurus (to reduce ego) is the only thing that can take us across this ocean of the spiritual ego. When the mind has been dissolved from its own sense of ego, the Self will radiate from within.

Meditative living brings silence, harmony, peace, purity of thought, alertness, and simplicity. The simple and innocent mind, like a child, can feel pure love, can see beauty, can be warm, and compassionate.

We can Be instead of trying to Become.

---

[16] Vairagya (Sanskrit)

Meditative Living is pathless and in the moment. It is here and now, without preference and prejudice. It is in tune with the Truth, with Cosmic Intelligence, and enjoys the freedom of Life in the midst of worldly living. This then is true meditation.

Meditative living is the seventh and final step of the journey!

Inspiration for Enlightenment

Choosing this book to read means that seeds of spiritual knowledge have been sprouting in your heart: seeds from many past lives. Spiritual seekers know that there is something more to living than earning money, consuming, and enjoying it. They are aware of a wider angle, and a subtler dimension of a different, indescribable world. Experiences and moments in solitude and extreme beauty make us aware of this other possibility. There is no other explanation than past lives, for each and every thought of ours has a cause and a reason. Picking up this book, then, is no accident; it is the design of the Universe. Your path is your past desire now coming to fruition.

The gurus and rishis scattered lessons through the ages for all to catch, but not all grasped the true inner meanings of their profound wisdom.

To reach enlightenment is the final blessing from the Universe. It is the culmination of numerous past lives of yearning, learning, and living in spiritual fullness. I cannot call it an "achievement", for many things can be achieved in life; and one achievement follows another. Rather, enlightenment is the final destination, nothing ever to be achieved again. Not in this lifetime or the next. This is moksha, literally translated "liberation." So splendid and majestic this moksha is said to be! So wondrous is Consciousness, so inviting in its purity and fullness, without which Pure Love cannot be known. For happiness, joy, peace, and calm are the forerunners and foundations of Universal Love and Freedom.

Enlightenment is Self-Realization. The literal meaning of self-realization is Realization of the One Consciousness, the Self, and the simultaneous departure of the relative world. One can exist psychologically in the Absolute and physically in the relative world. Since thoughts are responsible for our actions, mental dissipation of desires is a natural outcome of Spirituality. Not all of us wish to become monks; rather, we want monkhood.

In earlier stages of spirituality, happiness equals desires fulfilled divided by desires entertained. In later stages of our spiritual journey, however, we realize that we are happiness itself, and the desire to "become" happy through obtaining, doing or being something vanishes. We get closer and closer to moksha. Putting it yet another way, when love for Liberation develops in our heart, desires inevitably fall by the wayside.

Life will never be the same again for those who will come to have glimpses of the Truth. We discover the purpose of life, the impetus for living. We perceive the Fullness of Life, and walk the pathless path to Joy and Liberation. Like rain-petals falling from the heavens, Grace showers on us when we realize that *if we do our part, the Universal Consciousness will take care of the rest. Through Cosmic Governance, it is made certain. There is absolutely no doubt about that.*

Achieving perfect purity of the Heart and absolute knowledge of the Self is the only way to Enlightenment or Moksha. Having accomplished this, the mind drops off and the ego dissolves. No more the push and pull from the world is experienced. Present is the only Reality where the past and future are left behind in the playground of the mind. No karma is formed from a sense of egohood, and the Realized Self is beyond both free will and destiny, beyond time and space. The Realized Self is inherently the Brilliant Blissful Consciousness.

Let us pray and meditate to reach the spiritual pinnacle of our journey. Let the path be as clear as the cloudless night and as illumined as the night of the full moon. Let me walk the path boldly to reach where few have the stamina to go, to reach where countless strive to mentally dissolve their bondages with the world. Let the path be doubtless and the destination clear. Let me rest awhile with the saints and sages on my way. Let me bow my head in reverence again and again for their teachings. Let my head never lift up in vain. Let my humility be such and adoration so complete. Let every word uttered by the ancients be a drop of nectar in my Ocean of Wisdom, collected painstakingly with tears of joy.

Knowledge alone has set me free from this world, this samsaar.[17] Truth is my name and Beauty is my formless form. Let me hasten my way through life towards immortality. Let dewdrops and rain roll off this Lotus Heart of mine. Pure or impure, whatever I may be, always meditating on the Lotus Heart, let me become Pure.

Asatomah sat gamaya: Lead me from untruth to Truth

Tamsomah jyotir gamaya: Lead me from darkness to Light

Mrityormah amritam gamayah: Lead me from mortality to Immortality

Om Tat Sat

---

[17] Samyak charati iti samsaar (Sanskrit).

A Practical Guide to Starting the Journey

Applying spiritual concepts to daily living is the ultimate challenge. Day to day problems overwhelm us. Our busy lifestyles do not allow us the time to reflect. Many of us do not even realize what is happening to us, though we know from time to time, usually in our quieter moments, that we remain unfulfilled. We suddenly realize that we want something more out of life.

Let us recap the seven steps of our spiritual journey:

1. The first lesson is to discover that you are the Spirit living in the body.

2. The second lesson is to understand that God exists as Existence-Consciousness-Bliss (Brahman); and the Spirit in you (Atman) is none other than this "God" at the microlevel.

3. Understanding that there is order in the Universe in the form of Pure Intelligence is the third major milestone of our journey.

4. The fourth lesson is to understand that the delusory power of maya takes us away from Truth and Permanent Happiness, and does not allow us to experience who W*e* really are.

5. The fifth lesson is to know that karma exists and what you do today determines your tomorrow.

6. The sixth lesson is to follow dharmic principles to alleviate the effects of karma.

7. Living a meditative life of awareness is the final step of the journey! Intensity of intent will determine the course to Enlightenment.

Understanding of these truths will build a strong foundation for more in-depth learning in later stages. However, knowing spiritual concepts intellectually is only the first step. Practicing the philosophy is what is required for happiness and freedom and eventually, if one craves, enlightenment. Let us proceed to see how we can apply these subtle concepts.

First of all, we must keep top of mind certain truths:

- We are looking for happiness and that is the goal. All else is a means.

- Our goal is freedom from suffering. Alleviation from suffering is achieved through spiritual knowledge and practice.

- A change in attitude is required. The way we think needs to change at the most fundamental level. To change our way of thinking, we must be convinced that the philosophy makes sense. Only then can we believe it, own it, and live it.

- Tremendous strength and courage is required to walk this path of spiritual practice because it requires us to act without compromising our knowledge or ideals.

Applicability in daily life should be approached at two levels: (1) externally at the level of lifestyle, and (2) internally at the level of the mind. Practices on both fronts are provided below and should be used to guide our interactions with the world and to unlearn and free the mind.

Lifestyle: Getting our lifestyle in order

- Make an altar in your home where you can meditate for ten minutes everyday. Make sure it is a quiet spot that creates beauty and harmony for the senses. Candles, flowers, incense, music, etc., will keep the senses engaged and free from distraction. Starting your day in this manner will help you get through the day.

- Meditate, but know how and what to meditate on. Meditate in your own way; there is no particularly right and wrong way. As time moves on, a sense of calmness will develop automatically.

- Do one action at a time, deliberately and slowly. This will slow down your thoughts and make you actively aware. Contrary to time management techniques, multitasking takes away the simplicity of life and therefore encourages anxiety and stress.

- Stay in the present moment with all your focus on the job at hand. This means not thinking about the past or future during the concentrated activity. This too will start to happen automatically once you become aware. You will be amazed at how productive you are!

- Handle everything with great reverence. All things such as books, chairs, food, clothes, trees, should be revered. Think in this way: books are precious because they provide knowledge, food is precious because it provides sustenance, clothes are precious because they shelter our body, furniture is made from wood and wood is precious for so many reasons. All in the world is precious; let us be grateful.

- Accept the changing nature of the body with age. This is bound to happen since it is part of the wheel of life. Let us revere age for experience culminates in wisdom.

- Start getting rid of clutter around you, and start the process of feeling free of psychological clutter. Outside clutter is a sign of mind clutter. The yogi does not live a complicated life, and possessions only complicate life.

- Balance your external lifestyle with the internal. Spend at least one hour of the day recharging yourself through an uplifting or meditative activity such as walking, listening to music, reading uplifting material, discussing spirituality, being in association with good people, etc. Over time, as you begin enjoying this downtime, your time will naturally shift towards peaceful activities.

- Follow a good role model. Find several people in history or real life who provide inspiration and allow them to uplift you and provide you the mental nutrients you need.

- Distance yourself from disagreeable situations and people as much as possible; befriend like-minded people who can energize you with positive thoughts until you are grounded. Then you can offer a positive environment to others yourself.

- Time is precious and should be invested towards your growth. Using time for lateral or purposeless movements in life will not allow you to move on.

- Change in life is good; it allows one not to stagnate and creates opportunities for growth. Welcome changes as they come and draw on them for spiritual growth.

The Mind: Getting our mind to work for us

- Don't try to conquer the world: conquering your mind is conquering the world. One cannot change the world to suit oneself. We will spend unnecessary energies on manipulating people and environment. Rather, learn to ride the wave and focus on changing from within. Develop inner strength and move beyond the reach of the external world. The world will be a disturbance until you know *how* to handle it.

- Don't turn thoughts into action unless they move you forward towards your goal. Set two different goals. One, your inner psychological goal: what you want your mental state to be (if this is hard to do, use the goal of long-term, permanent happiness as a definition); and two, your external goals around finance and leisure. Any action that you take should move you forward on both accounts. You should feel harmonized in moving forward with both of these goals. If there is a conflict, give your inner goal priority, and let it guide your external efforts.

- Live mindfully of your "personal reality." The world is in the mind. Your reality is only personal to you. Understand what this means (chapter on The Mind) clearly and do not get enchanted or deluded by falsehood. Everything is simply neutral. We are the ones that put good and bad labels on things.

- Stop the running commentary in your mind. Do not make judgments. If it snows, say, "It is snowing." Do not say, "Why must it snow again!" Don't whine, because it is not going to change.

- Look at everything in the context of the larger picture. It definitely makes living easier! A larger perspective makes our own troubles look small. After all, we complain about very small things when many others suffer in much worse ways.

- Understand that everything is temporary. Change is inevitable on all fronts, and things will come and go. They always have and they always will. As you start to appreciate the precariousness of worldly things, you will naturally let them go. Their charm will continue to diminish the stronger your understanding becomes. So do not get attached to anything unless you are prepared to let it go one day.

- Accept the nature of objects and beings around you as they are right now. It is part of the universe, part of the laws of Reality. Say to yourself, "This is the way they are." When the filter of the mind is clean and pure, all things will be understood. Until then, if you cannot accept it, ignore it. If you cannot ignore it and have to take sides, ensure you are following dharmic actions. If you do not know what dharmic actions are, follow great role models.

- When bad emotions come, negate them through the understanding that they are temporary. Ask, "Who is feeling bad?" Reflect and assert the Real You. Keep asking, "Who am I?" If you make a practice of thinking that we are spiritual beings encased in a body, you will find that your mind will become accustomed to treating all as spiritual beings. This will eventually make the mind positive, subtle, and pure.

- Shift your vision from the outside to the inside. Uplift yourself at every opportunity. When you uplift yourself you will automatically uplift humanity.

Keep in mind that not all points are applicable to every situation. Like lanes on a road, these guidelines are intended to keep us on track.

Relevance in Everyday Life

Imagine waking up cheery every morning, starting your day with a calm mind, going about your work in a pleasing, pleasant manner and tone, insulated from the mad, rushing world and functioning at your own psychological pace. Imagine going through the day with a keen sense of passion and purpose, knowing that you are on solid ground. Imagine the evenings being spent with those whose love is real and can be felt, heard, and seen. Can we create that atmosphere? It is magical, but there it is, it can be done and *should* be done simply because it *can* be done.

On the contrary, imagine a life full of noise and frustration, anger and resentment, loneliness and depression, where moods and situations make it difficult to live in harmony and give and receive love. How, then, can we be at peace? Love, after all, is the basis for peace and happiness.

When we love one other person, only that one other person returns our love; but when we gain inner strength, we love the whole world. That is the difference between Universal Love and personal love. Ultimately, Universal Love will free us from all knots of the mind and heart.

Whether we are fourteen or ninety-four; whether we are single, married, divorced, or widowed; whether we are a mother, a father, or an aunt or uncle;

whether we are an employee or the boss; whether we are the repressed or the oppressed; or whether we sweep floors or we sit in executive chairs, the Self can be realized by all. There are no limitations anyone can put on any of us. There is no power that anyone can have over us in the spiritual world, for it is internal to us and needs no ones sanction or validation. The state of a spiritual mind is effortlessly shielded from interference, bringing immense inner strength regardless of circumstances. We are free to think and do.

Everyday from then on can be more enjoyable, satisfying, fulfilling, and positive for you and the ones around you.

The trick for gaining permanent happiness is to invoke the spiritual path everyday until it becomes second nature. Below is a very simple way of thinking about spirituality. When you feel depressed, stressed, or down, use this understanding to pick yourself up:

I am frustrated and tired today. How do I become happy?

By understanding that the mind is the one that is creating havoc. Inside me I am tranquil.

So how do I control the mind?

I don't need to control the mind. I need to understand the way the mind works. I need to understand that I have been conditioned to think in a certain way. I have to stop judging by the standards I have always used.

But I don't know what action I should be taking.

Firstly, be unbiased by understanding that you are beyond taking sides. When you are not being pushed or pulled, there are no frustrations. Things are as they are.

Secondly, any action taken should move me towards my goals. If you are in an unfavorable situation, tell yourself, "I am in a situation where I am not being treated properly. I must fight to uphold my dharma." Then move forward with courage and conviction and bask in the knowledge that you are being true to yourself. If you are secure and in a favorable position, say to yourself, "The primary goal in life is to live a life free of suffering. Everything else is a means. Let me always uphold dharma; and in that way, I will continue to boost my inner strength." Focus within and reflect on the Self to gain peace and happiness. Even the masters say it is the only way.

How do I focus on the Self? How can I gain tranquility?

Tell yourself, "I am the Spirit, same as the Universal Consciousness. As the Spirit, I am absolutely pure and free from any noise or distractions. My true nature is tranquility. My nature is not frustration, stress, or anxiety that has been brought on by the outside world and by my mind. They are "unreal" and brought on by maya. Let me be who I am supposed to be. Put into continuous practice chants and mantras that invoke the inner Self, e.g., "I am the eternal Spirit, intelligent, free, and pure."

How can I be sure that I am the Spirit?

Because the Consciousness inside me is what "I am." The "I" in me cannot be denied; otherwise, I would not be alive and could not even ask the question. If I see a dead person, he has the same body as I do, but he does not have the Spirit. I know there has to be, without doubt, two separate entities—the body and the Spirit.

But I might die before I am able to gain happiness.

No. You will never die. Your subtle body never dies whether you have a car accident, a fatal disease, get mugged and murdered, or die of simple old age. You will be transferred to another body to fulfill your remaining desires and exhaust your vasanas. All your desires will be fulfilled—it is part of the universal design.

When you are Pure Spirit, no one can harm you. You are eternal, infinite. All things happening to you are merely on a relative basis and mean nothing in the long term. The only objective in life is to evolve.

Yes, but why am I in this situation? I get angry and irritated when I think about my circumstances.

Why get irritated? Given enough time, things change—nothing is forever. You are where you are due to Universal laws. The law is bigger than you. And if you think someone is ahead of you, it is only now and in this lifetime. Don't worry. Universal Intelligence takes all into consideration. Put in as much self-effort as possible, and do your best according to universal values; then, let the Universe take its course. If nothing happens, keep trying anyway with a cool mind. Remember that when things happen easily, they are meant to be. When things take time to happen or never happen, it is because they were never meant to happen in that way—some other goodness will happen instead.

In any case, remember that your troubles are relatively small when put in the context of a larger picture.

And, if by chance you are doing well, don't get arrogant or take things for granted either. You could be in someone else's shoes tomorrow.

How am I to live?

By understanding that both the world and our minds are limited, relative, and illusory. Don't take anything too seriously except your own evolution. Do what you must to evolve spiritually, emotionally, and materially, in that order. Keep trying and don't give up. Understand that Extreme Intelligence is at work and will do the right thing through Cosmic Governance. Carry on doing what you are doing but with an attitude of gratefulness. Accept that you are where you are graciously, not grudgingly. You are there for many reasons. Learn, evolve, and keep moving upward and onward.

What then?

Then one reaches freedom and fulfillment. Fulfillment is about faith and attitude: faith in the fact that what is happening to us is intended, that no one can swerve and avoid happenings. With the attitude of true acceptance and receiving whatever comes our way as a sacred blessing, we continue up the spiritual path.

Unlike postponing happiness to the future, we can realize the Self right now, this second. How? I only need tell you that you are the intelligent Consciousness principle, not Jane or John Doe. It is here and now we can go though this transformation. But habits die hard. What if someone came and told you that you are not Susan Cheng? That at birth you were switched and you are really this other Susan who comes from some remote town west of the mountains? Would knowing that be enough to change who you love, how you live and what you do? No! Habits die hard and therefore we must practice.

How do I know I am making progress in gaining inner strength and developing a spiritually oriented personality?

The test is that you yourself will feel it. Sometimes others will notice a change in you, but really speaking, no one need know of your development. Your own success is your own gain, your own personal knowledge.

Spiritual evolvement does not necessarily mean that we will never get angry or greedy or feel hurt, etc. Rather, our evolution should be measured by how quickly we are able to catch ourselves reacting to these negative emotions.

Many times, people will behave as if they are spiritually evolved, but you think they do not really believe or embrace it. Ignore them; it is not our business. We should not be judging in any case.

Thinking in this manner will surely transform your attitude and your life over the course of time. When we start rising above relative matters and live in the Truth, everyone around us benefits. Like the fragrance of a rose, positive attitudes spread everywhere and take hold. Delightful vines twine around others to take root and blossom with the flowers of spiritual living. Ancients say that the proliferation of this glow and fragrance to others is certain.

We can all do our part in uplifting humanity.

Relevance to Corporations and Working Professionals

From the point of view of the corporation, the individual needs to display high performance, initiative, productivity, innovation, efficiency, etc. From the point of view of the employee, the culture imbibed by the corporation should foster trust, inspiration, encouragement, caring, etc. In a perfect world, we would not need government regulations, corporate compliance, diversity councils, and other protective and legal measures. But the world of maya (illusion) plays on the minds of individuals, both employees and employers. The relative world pulls and pushes people's desires, motivations, thoughts, and actions; and inevitably conflicts are created in many pockets of even an apparently healthy organization.

Spiritual wisdom can play a great role in the divergent needs of the individual and the corporation. The basic premise of any business is to serve their customer with a particular product or service while making profit. I believe that if customers and employees are satisfied, profits will invariably come.

After more than twenty-five years of experience in the corporate world, I truly believe that corporations that buy into a value culture and are able to propound it will always have an edge in longevity, sustainability, hiring and retaining staff, in customer loyalty, in competitive leadership, etc. The challenge is that values are subtle and not easy to implement. To shift to a value-based culture (human values as opposed to profit-based values) not only takes an inordinate amount of time and effort but is contingent on the inner strength, stamina, willpower, and patience of top management. Driven through inspiration and faith in mankind alone can such a superhuman shift of culture be undertaken.

Organizations measure individuals at two basic levels: hard skills and soft skills. Hard skills are those required for performing the job at hand while the soft skills reflect the attitude with which the individuals perform their job. Values play the leading role in the propagation or betterment of soft skills, which keep the psychological state of an organization healthy at both the micro and macro levels. Individuals who can grasp spiritual concepts and apply them to work life will have great advantages such as increased productivity, better teamwork, higher emotional intelligence, self-motivation, clarity, and self-awareness.

Many spiritual concepts can be applied to the workforce. Employers and employees can use the list of spiritual concepts laid out below to their advantage.

Vision

Set your vision high. When we think at the highest levels, we forget ourselves, thereby reducing our egos. We must think that we are working for a cause (which could be the product we produce or the service we provide). When two children fight, it is the mother that stops the fight because the mother is working from a higher viewpoint while the children are focused on their egoistic needs.

Goals

Be clear that happiness is the goal, and work is a means to the goal. If you rely consistently on the job for your happiness, remember that happiness generated from the external world will be intermittent. Rather, do work that you enjoy—that you have an aptitude for. If you have the aptitude for the work you do, you will not only enjoy it but be good at it. Follow your swadharma[18], and start to eradicate your vasanas.

Achievement

Self-actualization is an innate need at higher levels of achievement orientation. By all means, have a desire to grow in your career. But remember that all is temporary. Each job should be a learning experience from which you move forward in the journey of life. The many jobs that we undertake will one day come to an end, but the learning we acquire will be permanent. It is the knowledge and success gained that brings a sense of achievement. What is the use of growing up the ladder for its own sake? Remember power and status are temporary. We want to focus on achievement not from a power perspective but from an inner-fulfillment perspective. It is better to be known for what you are good at rather than to have a reputation for your incompetence or to gain unjustified recognition.

Emotional Intelligence

From a spiritual standpoint, emotional intelligence means that at all times one is able to deal gracefully with all situations. Accept circumstances as they change, for change is inevitable and should be welcomed. Be patient and tolerant and learn to ride the wave. If your coworker gets ahead of you, remember it is karma playing its role; don't take it personally. If you feel you have been treated unfairly, fight for your dharma by all means and continue to do your best. If the fruits of the effort come, well and good; if they do not come, make a decision whether to move on or not and perform that action. Do not complain endlessly to yourself or others; it will only bear negative results. Try not to be a management challenge in that context.

---

[18] Your own dharma or what is natural to you (Sanskrit).

Teamwork and Conflicts

Keep dharmic values like fairness, reverence, trust, kindness in mind. Do not judge others: who are you to judge? Ignore those who judge you: who are they to judge you? Judging is the result of the conditionings of our minds. Tell yourself they do not know any better, and nor do you. This will make you open to new concepts and ideas, and being open will also allow you to generate more ideas and be innovative. It will also make you appreciate your colleagues.

You may think you can do someone else's job better than they can. Chances are you do not know what that job entails. Putting yourself in others' shoes is easier said than done. Each job has its own pressures.

Fairness, Equanimity, and Truthfulness

By far, justice and fairness are the most important attributes for each individual to uphold. This is especially true for those in position of leadership roles. It is the underpinning for trust and loyalty. Management is judged heavily by staff on fairness. There can be no hidden agendas at play.

Trust

Ensure you have no hidden agenda. Only then can people trust you. If your hidden agenda is to be better than your teammate, then they cannot trust you. Hidden agendas are usually personally motivated agendas for recognition or advancement and, though not visible directly, can be perceived by others easily. Instead, develop an attitude of helpfulness so that the work at hand may get done faster and better. In that way, one can develop trust.

Professionalism and Personal Excellence

Society expects that the professionals who service their community are giving correct advice and guidance for the best service possible to their clients. This means that they take responsibility for the expert advice for the service offered. Service should be timely and commensurate with what the client is paying you to do. The client is buying a service for something they cannot or do not want to do themselves. No one can be their own doctor, lawyer, barber, banker, fitness instructor, teacher, etc.; so we must be the best at what we do. We must also be watchdogs and protect those who are relying on us from a governance perspective. This means that if you see someone doing something wrong in your profession, you have an obligation to rectify it. Do your part in society.

Accountability

Dharmic principles entrust that you take responsibility for your actions. When given a role, ensure you fulfill it to the best of your ability. People are relying on you and have chosen you for that specific job. Be responsible in fulfilling your duties at work.

Clarity

Be clear about your professional goal. Once you have established the goal, let every thought and action move you towards that goal. Be in the present moment to do the best job on whatever it is you are working on. Sharpen your concentration skills through meditation.

Ability to Draw Out the Essence

A sister attribute of clarity is the ability to rise above the details to ensure the right things are being done. Delve into details only when necessary; otherwise, they will consume you with every engagement. With limited time these days to get everything done, focusing on the essence is not only practical but is essential. This skill gets more important the higher you get in your organization.

People Management

As an employer, all relationships should be dealt with fairly, warmly, and with directness. Employees look for justice and support. Give it by being unbiased. If your swdharma is to manage and lead, only then should you take on people responsibilities. It is not suited for all personalities.

Self-Awareness and Personal Control

This attribute will come easily once spiritual concepts are well understood. Understanding the play of the mind is pivotal to self-awareness. The mind can then help "lift oneself by oneself."

Managing for Inclusion

Seeing oneness in all beings is a natural outcome of spiritual learning. Our minds have been conditioned by society to like and dislike due to differences and comparisons of "I" and "mine." If our minds can go beyond these differences, it becomes easier to accept others.

Time Management

Do not waste your own time or others' time. Get to the point quickly. Focus your energies on the purpose or objective, not on the people. Meditation helps efficiency through concentrated focus. Ensure work-life balance no matter what level you are. You need to nurture your personal self and energize your batteries daily, so you can maximize your intelligence and skills from nine to five.

Act, Don't React

Take a fresh view on everything. Understanding that the mind is conditioned to elicit a certain response, change the way you judge and evaluate. Be more objective by being unbiased and act from values not personal agendas. Avoid acting from repeated behavior patterns.

Change

Understand that without change all things would be stagnant. Our bodies change, the weather changes, the wheel of life carries on. All things need to change in order to grow. Companies also need to grow and evolve. You may not understand the changes from a larger perspective so accept them and keep working your best.

Courage

Get fear out of your system by doing the right thing. When you do the right thing, the fair thing, no one can blame you. Doing the right things gives you inner strength, and conversely, not doing the right thing compromises your integrity. If others are not doing the right thing, take solace in the fact that karma is at play and will be at play in the future too.

Summary:

Understand what it is you love to do and what you are really good at. Each of us has specific strengths accompanied by a special personality. Bring your core personalities to work. Apply your passions to gain a sense of accomplishment. It could be your ability to help, your ability to share or motivate or lead or listen or organize or debate or push the envelope or reconcile. You could be a change agent or have the ability to influence, negotiate, sell, manage, and create, etc. A job is a job, but it is your personality that will make the difference. Find your niche, go for it, and do your best.

Whatever happens, keep in mind that you cannot control the outcome: *the outcome is not in your hands.* You can and should put in all the effort, but in the end, laws of the universe are more powerful than you. So apply those positive traits in you. Put your energy, your potential, your core personality, your individual strengths to work. And don't say you do not have them, because even your mother has been telling you your strengths and weaknesses since early childhood. They have not disappeared over time, so follow your swadharma. It is better than trying to fit into the shoes and clothes of another. When you follow your swadharma it allows your mind to be quieter and more available for inner development.

Change the way you measure your life and your worth. Economic advancement is one path, but inner development has more worth. Do not focus all your energies on power, achievement, success, and status while discounting the other. Spiritual development gives us inner strength to survive the most difficult of challenges through life, including the daily struggles at the workplace. It is what prepares us for life in general. If we cannot develop our spiritual and emotional intelligence, we will quarrel with one and all, forget our responsibilities, stay scattered and angry, demotivated, and unproductive. What good can you be to any organization under those circumstances?

Organizations can differentiate themselves by adapting a culture that promotes a healthy work environment. In recent years, instant communication capabilities, globalization, and a 7*24 culture has created an unhealthy pressure for time, and a stressful and frustrated corporate lifestyle for many employees. The younger workforce has smartened up and is searching for more meaningful and fulfilling work, and retired employees are beginning to take on new social and humanistic ventures.

Only through a values based corporate lifestyle can we influence transformational success for the majority of the working population.

My Story

It has been ten years since my son's and husband's deaths, since the storm that altered the lives of my daughter and I: as if God's huge hand watchfully lifted two tiny people from a terrible earthquake and placed them on new ground. New fertile ground that needed to be nurtured, consoled, forgiven. Appeasing the mind whenever it threw a tantrum and painstakingly correcting its inaccuracies and its headstrong presumptions. New raw emotions emerged, new ways of thinking in new circumstances.

And sometime after the deadly incident, there was new hope. Like a newborn sprout struggling to be free, we entered a new expansion.

In the ten years, lofty lessons have been imparted to us. We understood all as the will of the Universe. What we have, we realized, is far more important than what we do not. We also realized that our lives, values, beliefs, and our spirit are far more valuable and require more gratitude than all our personal possessions put together, for subtle expressions and experiences are felt more acutely than any experience in the material world.

Every life experience for me has been a lesson. Not in morality, but in recognition of the fact that each experience is in itself a juncture, a significant play that occurs at the right moment with the right people, to shape me into what I am today. It matters not who; it matters not whether the incident was pleasant or unpleasant. It is the incidents themselves and their impact on me that are significant in the play of life.

I must cherish *all*, for *everything* has its contributions. And in striving to live, I must ensure that the fabric of my outer self is in complete harmony with the richness of my inner texture. It is not worth living unless I live meaningfully.

The old past now feels as though it never existed: it is some far-off dream that took place aeons ago, a long-forgotten journey that takes an effort to recall, to connect with. I forget the faces, the animations, the words, the specific incidents. Only the soft intuitions remain: the way I feel, the movement of my heart as it tries to grasp a new situation and lets it go suddenly, instinctively, with the effects of a pensive appreciation for the ongoing drift of life. What sustains, then, is the belief in something so much more powerful than ourselves.

Let my mind wander now to a trip that happened eight years ago at the foothills of the Himalayas. It was the journey to Gomukh, the very abode of the Lord, the place high in the mountains where Gods live. The glacier starts high in the Himalayas, from which the sacred river Ganga commences her flow. The Holy Ganga water is said to purify the Heart. I had taken my sons ashes there to give him the purest, most precious rite of all so that his right of passage could be nothing else but noble and sacred.

Gangotri, a small town, stays open between May and October. It is situated at approximately twelve thousand feet. At one time, the glacier had started melting here. Now it has receded some fifteen kilometers inward and risen two thousand feet higher. The sacred journey starts at Gangotri and winds its way to Goumukh, the mouth of the glacier. The way upward feels like a beautiful musical crescendo waiting to be heard.

We start from Gangotri at 5:00 a.m. There is me, my cousin, our guide, and the local Sherpa. It is still dark. I can smell the daybreak in the moisture of the wooded trees. Here, amongst the highest mountain peaks, is an unmatched tranquility, a holy elegance. The Divine Force is evident in every breath, every step, every blade of grass, and every particle of Earth. Here the trees whisper their prayers as they sway ever so slightly, the clouds bow their heads low, the mountains join their hands, and the wind scatters its flower offerings in loose petals and leaves. I see the first sunrays slowly, steadily offering their *arti*[19] to the World. I am filled with joy to be part of this wonder. And here, the new day, a new Miracle, comes alive in a slow trance, bewildered by its own beauty. There is no ego here, only humility layered upon humility: so much humility that I have to beg forgiveness for being human.

The path is no more than two to three feet wide with the mountain on one side and a deep gorge on the other. The Bhagirathi River, which meets with other tributaries and becomes Ganga, runs alongside, far below the winding trail. We cross three or four stands where hot chai and Indian bread is available. The route is speckled with streams that have to be crossed using rough logs, some still round but flattened from wear this season. The water is so pure that I can scoop it up with my cupped hands and quench my thirst. I must do that because I want Her, GangaMa, to be a part of me.

The way is safe for the most part, but instances present themselves. They are unnervingly life threatening. It is July monsoon, and I can see some of the paths worn down from new streams created by the rainwater. There are several occasions where the path is reduced to a foot in width, and where the ground is so weak from rain that I really am not sure if I will make it across. One slip and I'm gone; well at least it is God's abode! The local Sherpa holds my hand because I am not as sure as I imagine myself to be. The boulders by my side are so flat that

---

[19] An offering of prayer performed with a lighted oil lamp.

I cannot hold on to them. Faith and my son are giving me the courage to move on. And now that there is relief from the narrow paths; there is danger from the overhead, almost-vertical lime rocks. "Go slow," I tell myself, "so we don't create an avalanche from the disturbance of our vibrations."

We reach Goumukh around midday. We walk a kilometer negotiating stones and huge boulders and very large pools of cold, shallow water. The clear skies that had accompanied us now decide to give way to masses of gray clouds, and the overcast sky brings cool breezes and shivers. I clamber over more rocks, managing to gather some wild magenta flowers as part of the offering. I look for a quiet spot where I can reach the banks. Slippery rocks lie amidst the gray brown sand. Tufts of fine olive-colored grass are scattered here and there. It's quite magnificent. The sound of the water is forceful, almost deafening. I manage to slide to the edge of the spirited Bhagirathi, its energy crashing along the banks, striking the blue icebergs in gigantic heaps. On the other side of the river, I can see water trickling down the brown and white hills of stones.

I do not need a priest for the offering of flowers, mantras, and ashes. God will be happy enough with my own honest prayers.

Now when I need to touch God, I go to those holy mountains. There, the spirit soars to new dimensions. God is not elusive there: there I can catch Him easily; He can teach me lessons swiftly. There is a gentle smile of silent understanding when we stand face-to-face.

And when I come back into the world, I thankfully realize that my spirit cannot be captured and kept bound. I am free of the emotional clutter of a world heaped with conflict and confusion.

> Stone walls do not a prison make,
>   Nor iron bars a cage;
>   Minds innocent and quiet
>   Take that as a hermitage.

> If I have freedom in my love
> > And in my soul am free,
> Angels alone that soar above,
> > Enjoy such liberty.[20]

Writing this book has given me the power to seize the reins of this mad, rushing world in which we live and pull them back with all the strength that God has given me.

It would be presumptuous of me to think that I can lift humanity through this book; but at the very least, I can request you to pause and reflect on life. Look at the sum total of your life to date and look to the many years ahead. What have you done so far, and what do you want from the rest of your life? Take a couple of days off to search within. Life is precious. Don't waste a minute with the mundane. Instead, move forward boldly. The laws of the Universe beckon you and await patiently your profound journey within. Good luck!

---

[20] Richard Lovelace, "To Althea, from Prison"

Acknowledgements

My deepest thanks to all those who have inspired me into action through their silent encouragement and belief in me.

About RITA NAYAR

Ms Nayar has a university degree in psychology, is a senior corporate professional in Toronto's financial industry, and is an accomplished teacher and practitioner of the eastern philosophy of Vedantic tradition. She gained her mastery of Vedanta at the feet of invaluable Gurus at the Chinmaya Mission worldwide, among others.

Rita's unique background has given her the ability to seamlessly fuse the compassionate spiritual realm with the tough corporate world. Growing up in South East Asia, Europe, Africa and North America, she brings a unique blend of human understanding and a distinctive global perspective into her teachings.

The Happiness Quotient is Rita's second book. It is the force behind Rita's triumph over the cruel tragedy of her husband and son's murder suicide, which is covered in Rita's previous book, *Ordeal By Fire* (TSAR, 2003). This tale of unbelievable proportions won the "In Celebration of Women" Award in 2005. *Ordeal By Fire* can be found in Chapters, Indigo in Canada and online at amazon.com. Ms Nayar has been featured on CBC, CITY TV, OMNI TV, and other media for her previous writing.

Rita brings to the world profound learnings based on her extraordinary experiences and acute understanding of life. She was compelled to write this book for the thousands of men and women, young and old, who are searching greater fulfillment and want to reach a state beyond what today's chaotic, material, and competitive world can provide.

Rita lives in Toronto, Canada.

To book Rita Nayar for talks, seminars or satsangs, logon to

www.theHappinessQuotient.com
or
www.RitaNayar.com
or
email her directly at
Rita.Nayar@yahoo.com

Printed in the United States
111428LV00009B/72/A